THE ABCS OF RVING

EVERYTHING YOU WANTED TO KNOW
ABOUT RVING BUT WERE AFRAID TO ASK

CHUCK WOODBURY

RV TRAVEL

The ABCs of RVing, Third Edition

ABOUT RV TRAVEL

RV Travel can best be described as a community. It's a group of people of all ages who love to explore the world by RV.

Its heart is a very popular website, www.rvtravel.com, with news and information, and a newsletter that keeps the community up to date with the latest trends and happenings in the RV world.

Join us by clicking on the link below, and become part of our family. You'll be glad you did.

https://www.rvtravel.com/subscribe/

HOW TO READ THIS BOOK

Disclaimer: To the best of our knowledge, the information here is solid and our advice accurate. Others, however, may not agree with all of what we say, so please keep this in mind.

Use this information as a guide, and don't make a purchase or other major decision based solely on the paragraph or two you read here about a particular subject. If something is THAT important, be sure to check with other sources before making a major decision.

There is no reason that you must read this book from front to back. Browse through and look for subjects that you're interested in. We covered a lot here. Reading in bite-size chunks works just fine.

ABOUT THE AUTHOR

Chuck Woodbury is a legend in the RV world. In 1989, he founded the quarterly newspaper "Out West," which he published for 12 years while on the road in a motorhome as he traveled the American West.

Through the years, Woodbury and his unique periodical were spotlighted on ABC World News Tonight, The Today Show, CNN and National Public Radio, in addition to hundreds of periodicals including USA Today, People Magazine, MotorHome, the Washington Post and Los Angeles Times.

Woodbury is also the editor of one of the world's largest websites about RVing, RVtravel.com. He is also the host of the Better Business Bureau DVD "Buying a Recreational Vehicle." In 2013 he was honored as the Distinguished Journalist of the Year by the RV Industry Association. In a typical year he spends three months on the road with his 32-foot motorhome.

INTRODUCTION

When someone begins thinking of buying a recreation vehicle, many questions come to mind.

Some are so seemingly basic that one might be embarrassed to even ask them. But, to paraphrase the old saying, there are no embarrassing questions.

With that in mind, I've compiled the answers to more than 200 questions I've heard over and over again during my career writing about travel and RVing. They're the things that those new to RVing and the RV lifestyle most want to know.

Now I share them with you. Enjoy!

BUYING AND FINANCING TIPS

W hat's a recreation vehicle?
Although the term can be loosely stretched to include just about any vehicle that is used for recreational purposes, a recreation vehicle (RV) is generally a transportable, motorized or non-motorized vehicle that is used for temporary living and contains, at the very least, a bed for sleeping.

Most RVs, however, also contain a kitchen area, bathroom, dinette and often an area with a couch or other lounge chairs. Recreation vehicles are highly mobile, unlike mobile or manufactured homes, which are intended to be towed once to a location where they will serve as a home.

RVs are generally between 12 and 45 feet long, with most in the 15- to 35-foot range.

Is there a difference between a recreation vehicle and a recreational vehicle?

No. For years, the RV industry used the term recreational vehicle to describe its products. But in the early 2000s, it began using the term recreation vehicle instead.

What's the difference between a Class A, Class B and Class C motorhome?

Class A motorhomes are constructed on a specially designed motor vehicle chassis. They're the "Big Boys" of the motorized RVs, and are the most favored motorhome of full-timers. They are also generally the most expensive RVs with price tags of luxury models a half-million dollars or more.

Class A RV

A Class B motorhome is a compact unit that looks much like a regular van. These are popular because they can often be parked in the family garage or driven around town as a second vehicle. Per square foot, however, a Class B usually costs more than a Class C.

Class B RV

A Class C motorhome is built on an automotive-manu-
factured van frame with an attached cab. The motorhome
manufacturer completes the living section and attaches it to
the cab and chassis. A Class C motorhome is easy to identify: In most cases, a full- or queen-size bed extends over
the cab.

Class C RV

What's a travel trailer?
The travel trailer was the first popular RV. It's pulled by a
car or truck, comes in many lengths, weights and designs,

and is the biggest selling RV. In recent years, lightweight models have become popular in part because they can be towed with most passenger vehicles, even four-cylinder models.

Travel Trailer RV

What's a fifth wheel travel trailer?

A fifth wheel trailer is much like a conventional travel trailer except it is built with a raised forward section for a bi-level floor plan. Fifth wheels, which are very popular with full-timers, are pulled behind a pickup truck using a special hitch mounted in the truck's bed. They are very stable to tow and often very spacious inside. You'll sometimes hear them called "fivers."

They are so comfortable these days, and so relatively affordable, that many people are selling their homes and living in "fivers" year-round.

Fifth Wheel RV

What's the difference between a travel trailer and a fifth wheel trailer?

First, the travel trailer is perhaps the most traditional and best-known recreation vehicle, having been around far longer than motorhomes, fifth wheels or other RVs. Generally, travel trailers are also the least expensive RVs (except folding camping trailers) and can be pulled by most vehicles. The more powerful the tow vehicle, the longer (and heavier) the travel trailer that can be towed.

Because of the special hitch required, fifth wheel trailers can only be towed with a truck, whereas travel trailers can be towed by cars or SUVs (and even a motorcycle, in their very smallest versions). On the road, however, a fifth wheel trailer is more stable and more easily controlled in windy conditions.

Because the front section of a fifth wheel trailer hangs over the truck bed, the combined length of a tow vehicle and its trailer is shorter with a fifth wheel than the same size travel trailer.

.   .   .

What's a truck camper?

A truck camper is a recreation vehicle with the living area on the bed of a pickup truck. It's amazing how many features can be packed into these very comfortable units. Access to the living area from the cab is seldom possible, however.

The camper can be removed from the truck at the campground or back home, allowing travel in the truck without the weight and/or inconvenience of the camper unit. In recent years, truck campers have become nearly as comfortable as mid-sized motorhomes. Truck camper prices typically range from about $6,000 to $60,000 (plus the cost of the truck).

Truck Camper RV

What is a folding camping trailer?

Also called "pop up trailers," these canvas-covered RVs are great for family summer vacations when the weather is mild. They are also the least expensive RVs and can be pulled by smaller cars (even subcompacts) than those required for regular trailers.

As their name implies, folding camping trailers fold up for rolling down the highway. Once at the campsite, however, they are easily expanded into remarkably spacious RVs with most of the conveniences found in bigger units, including a porta-potty and even a shower in the largest.

Smaller units usually include one or two queen- or king-size beds, a sink and a 12-volt refrigerator, and a little bit of cupboard space. Folding camping trailers are often the first RVs of young families, and they provide many memorable vacation memories for children. Two hard-sided trailers that also fold for travel are the Aliner and TrailManor; however, more RV manufacturers are entering the hard-sided building race.

Folding Camper RV

I've heard about "toy haulers." What are they?

This term applies to RVs that have a rear bay designed for transporting ATVs, motorcycles or even cars. There is a full-width door in the back that opens down to serve as a ramp for loading vehicles. The rear bay is often equipped with options that enable it to be used as a spare room when not loaded with "toys."

Many are equipped with beds that are raised toward the roof while traveling, but can be lowered at bedtime. Toy hauler models are available in larger travel trailers and fifth wheels, and sometimes motorhomes. Sales of toy haulers have boomed in recent years.

Toy Hauler RV

What is a park model RV?

The RV Industry Association (RVIA) defines park model RVs as "a unique trailer-type RV that is designed to provide temporary accommodation for recreation, camping or seasonal use."

According to the RVIA, nearly 70 percent of park model RV owners locate their unit within several hours' drive time from their primary residence and use them for weekend camping trips.

Park models almost always remain in one place, rather than move from place to place like other RVs. They are more like small "mobile homes" than what most people consider a recreation vehicle. Another term the industry is beginning to use for these is "destination trailer."

Are tiny houses RVs?

No. They are not recognized by the RV Industry Association, and are not required to meet the manufacturing standards of traditional recreation vehicles. Although tiny homes are in the news a lot today, you rarely see them in RV parks or campgrounds.

Is there a single resource where I can read descriptions and specifications of new-model RVs?

The only printed source we're aware of is The RV Buyers Guide published annually by GS Media & Events, a division of Good Sam Enterprises. Look for it at large RV bookstore newsstands.

Where can I learn if my truck can tow my travel trailer?

Trailer Life offers an annual guide, the "Good Sam Guide to Towing." It outlines critical information about hauling travel trailers, fifth-wheels and truck campers. Visit https://www.trailerlife.com/trailer-towing-guides/ for a free guide.

What's a "slideout"?

A slideout is an option that allows RVers to expand the space inside their rigs once they reach their destination. At the touch of a button, a portion of a room — usually the living room or bedroom (or both) — slides out, up to about 3 1/2 feet.

Most RVs today, except small ones, include this option. Some units have two, three, four or even five slideouts and some Class A motorhomes have "full wall" slides.

The interiors of RVs with slideouts are so spacious it's hard to tell them from a regular home. It's best to avoid slide-outs that include the stove and refrigerator because of the weight which can put a strain on the slideout.

TIP: Before buying a particular RV with slideouts, be sure to see the RV with the slideouts fully retracted, as they will be on the road.

With some models, you won't be able to get to the bathroom, kitchen and/or bedroom, which would be very inconvenient when you wanted to pull over at a rest area to make lunch, use the bathroom or take a nap. We recommend you avoid buying these poorly designed rigs (which are fairly common).

I understand there are different ways that slideouts work? Are some better than others?

There are two types of slideouts, based on the type of equipment used to move them. Electric slides, generally found on smaller slideouts, use an electric motor for propulsion. They can be sensitive, so when buying an RV with an electric slideout, slide it in and out watching and listening closely. Hanging up while moving or making scraping or loud popping noises could indicate a problem.

Electric motors can fail on these units, and gears can need replacement. Hydraulic slides use a pump and fluids to move the slide in and out and are more complex in design than electric units. Their failure points include valves, pumps, and hydraulic line leaks. They're more often found on larger, heavier slideouts.

If a slide shows any signs of glitches when in use, it's best to get it looked at right away, rather than risk being stranded with a stuck slideout.

How many people do RVs sleep?
Four to six on average, but sometimes less and sometimes more. Some RV manufacturers tend to be "generous" when calculating how many people can sleep in their rigs. Always try out the sleeping situation in a rig before purchase if it's a critical issue for your needs.

How can a Class C motorhome sleep six people? I read the ads, but can't figure out where everyone would sleep.
Here's how: Two people can sleep in the cab-over bunk. The dinette area also makes into a double bed, so that's two more. If there's a couch, it will fold out into another double bed for another two people. That makes six. It's not roomy, but it works.

But keep in mind that a motorized RV that advertises that it sleeps six does not necessarily mean you should be traveling with six people aboard. Their combined body weight and belongings could put the RV well over its weight capacity (CCC), which could impact the RVs performance on the road, increasing the chance of an accident. An overloaded RV will also stress it and shorten its life.

Do RVs come with bunk beds?

Yes, some do, and it's a good use of space for families with young children. These RVs are sometimes called bunkhouse models. We recently came across a trailer from Heartland with two full-size bunks (so four double beds) that, with other beds, sleeps 14.

We have a lot of stuff. Which type of RV has the most storage space?

Class A motorhomes have the most capacity for motorized RVs, followed by Class Cs (space is very limited in Class B motorhomes). Larger units typically have more than smaller ones. If you are considering a towable RV, fifth wheels usually have more storage space than travel trailers of equivalent size.

Be sure when you consider storage space that you also consider how much weight an RV can accommodate. It's easy to overload an RV which, if done repeatedly, can shorten its life. And overloading can be dangerous to occupants as well.

Which RV is best for me: a motorhome, travel trailer or something else?

A motorhome is a good choice if you move around a lot with brief stays in each place; you won't necessarily need another vehicle for sightseeing or chores. If you need a touring vehicle, however, you can tow a small car or truck.

Keep in mind, it can be difficult to find a place to park with a large Class A motorhome. If local sightseeing is in your plans, having a small car or truck along can make life easier.

An advantage of a motorhome over a towable RV (trailer or fifth wheel) is that you have access to the interior of the unit while you're on the road. It's easy for the passengers to grab a quick snack, for example, or use the toilet in an emergency (although it's always best to pull off the road to do so).

A trailer or fifth wheel is often the best choice for full-timers because they can park it and then drive the tow vehicle for shopping, errands and sightseeing. For RVers who spend weeks or even months in one place, a fifth wheel or trailer is often the best choice.

Towable RVs are also much less expensive than motorized ones because there is no costly engine (and its maintenance).

A truck camper is an excellent choice if you already own a truck. You'd be surprised how many features are packed into these compact units.

For infrequent family camping trips, and for campers on a tight budget, a folding camping trailer is an excellent choice. These are the lightest and least-expensive RVs, and can be pulled behind a small to medium-sized car. However, they are not suited to cold weather camping.

Can I ride in an RV while it's moving?

Yes, in a motorhome or truck camper, but keep all seatbelts fastened. If a motorhome sleeps four, then it should have four seat belts. If it sleeps six, it should have six belts. However, except for rare occasions it is not legal to ride in a travel trailer or fifth wheel trailer.

We strongly advise you never allow any passengers to ride in them even if it's technically legal — too dangerous. If you have ever seen photos of a crashed trailer or fifth wheel with pieces of the RV scattered everywhere, you will likely conclude that allowing someone to ride in one when moving is a monumentally dangerous idea.

Which is best for my motorhome, a gas or diesel engine?

Every year, more RVers opt for motorhomes with diesel engines rather than gasoline engines, but both are popular. The advantages of a gasoline engine over diesel is primarily the price. The new super chassis (both Ford and GM) make gasoline engine motorhomes a great buy. Not only are they less expensive than diesel, but they have good carrying capacity. Also, oil changes and maintenance are less expensive with the gasoline models.

The diesel motorhome rides quieter, though, because the engine is in the rear on most, and it can hold much more cargo including heavier materials in the interior such as Corian countertops, china toilets, and so on.

Diesel models usually have super transmissions and exhaust brakes which make mountain driving a breeze. Prices for an oil change on a diesel motorhome are all over the map, but easily start at $200 and can run much, much higher.

Much depends on what's included in the change — oil and filters are essential, but lubing all fittings is important. Some truck stops will beat dealer prices hands down.

One of the biggest differences between a diesel coach and one powered by gasoline is the life of the engine. Expect about 100,000 miles tops with a gas engine, but 250,000 to 500,000 with a diesel. In addition, you can expect better fuel mileage with a diesel, although in most instances it will cost more per gallon.

These days, more and more full-time RVers are opting for diesel-powered motorhomes — almost exclusively in Class A models — and manufacturers have responded by offering entry level models in price ranges starting at about $140,000.

However, for RVers who don't expect to put more than 10,000 to 15,000 miles a year on a coach, a gas-powered unit may well be a better choice because of its lower price tag.

What is a "diesel pusher"?

A diesel-powered motorhome is one with a rear engine (diesel pusher), the standard setup on virtually all diesel-powered motorhomes. However, front engine diesel chassis are now becoming available, mostly the shorter Mercedes Sprinter chassis. Most gasoline engines, on the other hand, are in the front of the motor coach.

What is a "bumper puller"?

It's a slang term for a travel trailer, also known as a "bumper pull." These can be pulled with a common trailer ball hitch, for some lightweight trailers with the ball mounted on the bumper of a car or truck. Heavier trailers require a tow ball mounted on a hitch system, bolted or welded to the vehicle frame. Contrast these trailers to "fifth wheel" trailers, which require a special hitch mounted in a pickup truck bed.

How much do RVs cost?

The price varies considerably. A small folding camping trailer might sell for $6,000. Motorhomes are $45,000 and up with most gasoline powered ones in the $70,000 to

$175,000 range and diesels from about $150,000 to $400,000. We've seen many luxury motorhomes priced higher than a million dollars.

Travel trailers and fifth wheels typically cost less (often far less) than a mid-priced motorhome of the same length because there's no engine. Truck campers, which slide into an existing pickup truck bed, start as low as $6,000 and can quickly rocket to $55,000. Many first-time RVers buy a used vehicle, where there are often great deals.

Why is it that two RVs of the same size, with basically the same features and amenities, can vary so much in price?

In a nutshell, the higher priced unit is generally built better and will last longer, or, said another way, "You get what you pay for!" Much of the difference in price is not so obvious at first glance — the type and quality of the materials used and construction, the craftsmanship, the insulation in the walls, etc.

When buying an RV, it pays to look very carefully in the nooks and crannies of the unit to see how it's built. RV makers have practiced the art of the "bling," building RVs that look great, but are built quickly and cheaply out of eyesight.

How much of a price reduction can I negotiate with an RV dealer on a new RV?

First of all, never pay Manufacturer's Suggested Retail Price (MSRP). This is top dollar, a number pulled out of a hat by a manufacturer. If you pay it, you'll be the RV dealership's sucker-of-the-month.

This is a complicated subject, but you should be able to negotiate at least 25-35 percent (or more) off the sticker price if you have patience and know what you're doing.

Is there a best time to buy an RV?

If you're shopping for a new RV, a good time to negotiate a great price is at the turn of the model year. Dealers and manufacturers want those "old" RVs off the lots. Sad to say, not all manufacturers have the same time frame for when their new models come out. You may have to do a little research, which is easier if you have a specific brand in mind.

On a seasonal basis, winter is considered the best time to shop. Sales are down, particularly in the more northern parts of the country, and dealers are often keen to make a sale. You also may get a better deal shopping on the last day of the month, where a salesman or dealer may be motivated to meet or beat a quota.

What's a PDI?

RV dealers should perform a thorough Pre-Delivery

Inspection (PDI) on every RV that arrives from the factory. Some dealers will go through the RV carefully, looking in every nook and cranny to be sure everything is in order.

But some dealers will do practically nothing. Time is money. These dealers will take a quick look for anything obvious and that's about it. They figure they can sell the unit, and then fix what's wrong later under its warranty (in some cases this could take weeks or longer).

You may not know which type of dealer you're dealing with. We highly recommend you hire an independent RV inspector to look over your prospective RV whether new or used. This could be a local mobile RV technician or a trained RV Inspector who specializes in such work.

You can find a certified RV inspection service here: https://nrvia.org/locate/. If the dealer will not allow you to hire an independent inspector, then walk away.

A representative of the dealer will offer you the opportunity to do your own PDI, or walk-through, by showing you how everything in the RV operates, providing you the opportunity to ask questions about anything that concerns you, including any defects you may spot.

Be sure that you schedule plenty of time for this, take copious notes and do not let the dealer talk you out of demanding something be fixed before you sign on the dotted line.

Some RVers even record their walk-through on video for future reference — a great idea. Be thorough. Try every door and drawer, every switch and faucet, every latch and lock. Make sure you learn how everything operates.

If anything will need fixing or adjusting, be sure you get what needs to be done in writing and have the dealer sign it. There are also DVDs that illustrate how to use all the systems of an RV.

Give me a few tips about buying an RV that I might never consider.

Okay, a few things:

1. Check the locations of electrical outlets. Be sure they make sense.

2. Sit on the couch and lay on the bed. Is the mattress comfortable? Is there head support on the couch? You'll spend a lot of time in these places.

3. Pull the slides in and see if you can reach the stove, refrigerator and bathroom. In some cases you may not: You'll be out of luck at rest areas when you need your own bathroom or to make lunch.

4. Sit where you will watch TV. Do you need to twist your neck uncomfortably to see the screen? Will you be

close enough to see the action on the screen? Some manufacturers will put the seating area at the end of the rig, then
make you look clear across the kitchen to see the TV!

5. Sit on the toilet to be sure you can do so with the bathroom door shut, and stand in the shower to be sure you fit.

6. Never trust what a dealer or other seller promises you
if your gut tells you it's not true.

**I know the make and model of my RV, but my local dealer
wants $2,000 more than a dealer about 200 miles away?
Which should I buy from?**

You'll likely find that service issues are more easily dealt
with if you buy from the dealer closer to home. While both
dealers are theoretically set up to handle warranty work for
the manufacturer, RVers report that when they bought an
RV elsewhere, they find themselves waiting in a longer line
to get service work done at the local dealer, or even denied
service. It may not be fair, but that's the way it is.

And when buying a new RV, you can pretty much be
assured that you *will* encounter warranty service issues —
sometimes a lot of them. You'll need to crunch the numbers
and see if your money — and time — are worth the savings
associated with driving back and forth a distance to get the
bugs worked out.

A survey at RVtravel.com revealed that nearly 30 percent
of the readers traveled 300 miles or more to buy their RV.

**If I buy from an RV dealer locally and then have a
problem far away on the road, will the same manufacturer's dealer there agree to fix it?**

No. Unlike car dealers, where any dealer of your make of

car will agree to fix it, RV dealers have no similar policy. If you buy a Winnebago in Denver and break down in San Diego, the local Winnebago dealer there has no legal obligation to fix your RV.

What advice do you have on buying a used RV?

We highly recommend buying used. Buying a used RV is not really different from buying a used car. You might find a better deal from an individual, but you'll need to inspect the unit very carefully and thoroughly. If it's a motorized unit, you should have it checked out by a good mechanic.

If you're looking at used RVs at a dealer, keep in mind that the dealer probably has a lot of flexibility built into the asking price. It's still important to inspect the unit thoroughly and get the dealer to fix anything that isn't working correctly before you take possession.

How long will an RV be on the sales lot before it is sold?

It can be days, or weeks, months or even a year or more. Be sure when buying a new RV to ask how long it has been on the sales lot, and check the chassis and elsewhere for any signs of water leaks, rust or other environmental damage.

I am about to buy a new motorhome. I don't understand why it has 2,500 miles on the odometer.

Motorhomes are driven from the factory to dealers, which can account for the mileage. It may also have been driven to an RV show or two, as well, which will add additional miles. The warranty of the rig will begin at the odometer reading when you buy it, not at zero.

. . .

Can I trust that an RV salesman will tell me the truth?

Not necessarily. He/she will try to sell you the RV and as many add-ons as possible — an extended warranty, insurance, roadside assistance, tire protection, etc., which are high-profit items. Some salespersons are perfectly honest, but others will say just about anything to make the sale and then ramp up the price with additional products, often priced far higher than elsewhere. It's hard to tell the good ones from the bad ones.

Most salespeople are paid by commission, so they use whatever techniques they can to sell you an RV. Never buy on your first RV sales buying outing, no matter what the pitch. Do your homework. Take your time.

Do you have a quick tip about identifying a good salesperson?

Ask him or her if they currently own an RV or have in the past. If not, be cautious. Also, ask the salesperson how long he or she has been with the dealership: If it's been for years, that's a good sign.

Keep in mind, too, that the first thing a salesperson will do is try to earn your trust. He'll ask you if you have a dog. You say, "Yes." "Aren't they great?" he'll say, trying to establish common ground. He/she might ask, "Do you plan to bring your grandchildren along on trips?" and you'll say, "Oh, yes, I know they'll love it."

The salesman will say, "My grandkids love traveling with my wife and me," etc. The salesman knows what he's doing. He wants you to think of him as a friend, whose pitch you will then buy "hook, line and sinker." Be careful.

Are RVs expensive to maintain?

The automotive part of a motorized RV is just like any motor vehicle when it comes to service. Change the oil and perform other regular maintenance and they'll last for years. The living areas of RVs are no more work to maintain than a small home.

An RV does take some serious bouncing around, however, so things jar loose now and then. But a little puttering around with a wrench and screwdriver can usually keep this problem in check.

If you are totally "unhandy" you may not even want to buy an RV. Service can be hard to find. As RV technician and instructor Terry Cooper explains to his students, "Eighty percent of repairs can usually be done by the RV owner." Repair shops typically charge $150 an hour for labor. You'll save a lot by doing your own work.

What are RV shows and how can I learn where and when they are held?

RV shows are held throughout the country, usually in the first three months of the year and then again in the fall.

Some are far bigger than others, but all showcase a wide range of RVs sold by area dealers.

Vendors sell products and services, and RV factory representatives are sometimes on hand to expertly answer questions about their company's products. In addition, most shows offer free seminars on a wide variety of topics about RVing.

RV shows present a superb opportunity to leisurely examine a wide range of RVs and gather extensive information.

The biggest and best show in the United States is held each September in Hershey, Pennsylvania. Some tricky dealers will stage their own RV shows, but only with their own products. Don't get sucked into one of those buying traps.

Will I get a better deal buying an RV at an RV show than elsewhere?

Sometimes, but not always. You will almost certainly find RVs marked down at RV shows, and sometimes significantly — often as much as 30 to 35 percent of MSRP. But in most cases you can get the same price a week or two later at the same RV dealership.

It's best to attend an RV show to either start your research or add to it by inspecting your narrowed-down choices side by side. Never go to a show to buy an RV to take home. Salesmen will say whatever they can to make a sale to earn their commission and "spiffs" (bonuses to sell at the show).

Big dealers like Camping World will bring in special salespeople — all-stars who are experts at turning "lookers" into "buyers." They have every trick up their sleeve to sell to you right there and then. Don't fall for their pressure.

Overheard at an RV show we recently attended: Salesman to customer: "What can I do to get you out camping with this next week?"

What are the advantages and disadvantages of a wide-body RV?

The advantage of a wide-body is livability. There is more room inside these spacious units. The disadvantage is that many states have rules prohibiting wide-body RVs on at least some of their roads.

By wide-body, they mean the 102-inch-wide coaches, which are six inches wider than the standard-width RVs. Wide-body RVs can be driven on all Interstate highways, but going on the back roads in some states may be illegal.

Travelers who plan to spend a lot of time on secondary highways and two-lane back roads might want to stick to a standard-width RV (up to 96 inches wide).

.   .   .

Is it true that you cannot drive long motorhomes in certain states?

No, in the last couple of years all states have amended their laws to permit motorhomes of up to 45 feet in length. RVers with large trailers or fifth wheels should check with states where they plan to travel about combined length limitations. This site has state-by-state details: https://drivinglaws.aaa.com/tag/trailer-dimensions/.

Don't forget that if you want to visit national parks, some have length limitations, not based so much on law, but on practicality. Many older park campgrounds have short RV sites, narrow roads and tight corners.

How can I tell if there are any recalls on a used motorhome I'm considering buying?

Check out the National Highway Traffic Safety Administration's recall database at https://www.nhtsa.dot.gov/cars/problems/recalls. RVtravel.com publishes recalls as they are issued. Sign up to receive its free weekly newsletters at https://rvtravel.com/subscribe

My wife has a physical disability that makes it hard for her to get around in most RVs. Are there any RVs made especially for people who are physically challenged?

Yes. Winnebago makes a Class A motorhome for people with physical challenges. Check with your local Winnebago dealer. RVs are also great ways to travel for parents with disabled children who might not be able to conveniently travel otherwise.

For example, we know of an RVing family with a young

daughter who needs oxygen round-the-clock. With their motorhome, the equipment is easily transported along.

You should also contact the Handicapped Travel Club (https://www.handicappedtravelclub.com), which is a California non-profit corporation formed to encourage RV traveling for people with a wide range of disabilities. For free information, contact Mark Neurohr: 815-252-1868.

Is one manufacturer better than another?

There's no easy answer for this question, but here's a broadly painted one: Some people love a particular manufacturer or brand of RV while others think the same ones are junk.

Some say, "All manufacturers make good RVs, and all make crummy ones." Generalizing, we'll just say you get what you pay for: A cheaply built RV will not be as durable or last as long as a more expensive one. But that's not always true.

What are the biggest RV manufacturers?

The big three, which control about 80 percent of the market are Thor, Forest River and Winnebago. About 80 percent of all RVs are made in Indiana. Of those, about 65 percent are built in Elkhart County.

How are RVs financed?

Loans for new, large RVs typically range from 10 to 15 years, with some extending even 20 years. Whether the purchase is financed through a bank, savings and loan, finance company, credit union or RV dealer, most RV lenders require at least 10 percent of the purchase price as a down payment, and many prefer 20 percent down.

You will see offers of zero down, but never, never buy that way or you will be horribly upside down on your loan from the moment you drive off the sales lot. The better your credit, the wider your options of financing.

Our advice is never finance an RV for 15 or 20 years. And, by all means avoid loans longer than 10 years on inexpensive units. You will likely be upside down in your loan for the life of the loan, meaning if you want to sell the RV you will need to come up with cash to pay it off. That could perhaps be only $5,000, but on an expensive RV it could be $50,000 or more.

What does "getting upside down" mean?

This term refers to when a buyer makes little or no down payment on an RV (typically a new one) and stretches the payments for a lengthy term.

In essence, after a couple of years the value of the RV will have depreciated up to 40 percent or more while the balance on its loan has decreased far less.

For example, a two-year-old RV may have depreciated to a value of $60,000, but its owner may still owe $70,000 on its loan, meaning he will need to pay $10,000 just to get someone to take the RV off his hands. It's not uncommon to be $50,000 "upside down" on an expensive rig.

I'm not sure of my credit rating. How can I learn it before applying for a loan?

To see where you stand on your credit, you can get a free report from Annualcreditreport.com. It will include your credit score for all three of the major agencies: Equifax, Experian and TransUnion.

Generally, a good credit score for buying at the lowest interest is about 690. Many institutions look to see a credit score of 660 to 700 before offering a loan, but some will offer loans on credit scores as low as the 500 to 600 range, but beware of the high interest rates that may be charged!

I understand that I can write off the interest on an RV like it was a second home. Is this true?

Yes, as long as the RV is used as security for the loan and it must have basic sleeping, toilet and cooking accommodations.

The IRS publishes two booklets that contain helpful information on this subject. Copies of "Publication 936 — Home Interest Deduction" and "Publication 523 — Selling Your Home" are available by calling the IRS at 1-800-829-3676 [800-TAX-FORM] or online from https://www.irs.gov/publications.

Where should I get insurance for my RV?

Check with your present auto insurer if you're happy with the company or agent, but only if it offers policies specifically for RVs.

If you plan to live full-time in an RV, be sure your policy covers you: Many companies will not insure RVs used full-time (so read the fine print).

Two popular companies that cater to RVers are Progressive and Geico. Both, at the time of this writing, will insure full-time RVers.

.   .   .

Is RV insurance expensive?

Statistically, RVers are good drivers and insurance companies take that into account when setting rates. You will likely be surprised at the moderate rates.

I operate a business from my RV. Do I need special insurance?

It depends on who you ask. One representative from a prominent RV insurance brokerage told us they'd never heard of such a thing.

Another RVer reported he had a claim rejected when his insurance company ruled that because he made money from videos he monetized on YouTube, he was operating a business — which violated his policy.

It's best to ask any insurance company about its policy. And definitely get the answer in writing!

I've been told it's a good idea to get an extended warranty for my RV. What do you think?

This is a hot topic. Some RVers prefer to go without the extended warranty and take their chances on repairs that occur after their initial warranty expires.

Others believe that an extended warranty is a good idea, knowing they will never be stuck with a big repair bill. RV dealers push extended warranties because they earn a fat commission.

You will probably do much better shopping on the Internet for such a policy. Ask your RVer friends what they think. And be sure before you purchase an extended warranty to read every single line of the agreement.

One of the biggest complaints we hear about extended

warranties is that the warranty company will not pay for the cost of a repair. The company's usual claim is that the RVer violated the terms of his agreement where the fine print stated the repair requested was not covered.

But keep in mind that many if not most of the components in your RV have their own warranties — refrigerator, air conditioner, stove, heater, and in motorhomes the chassis and engine. Of course, all bets are off when buying a used RV — warranties tend to extend only to the original owner.

Where do I register an RV?
The same place you register your car.

Can I register my RV in another state to save money? I've heard that some states, like Oregon, have low fees.
Be careful! You'll need to claim residency for any state where you register. Penalties can be very steep if you get caught registering illegally.

Many full-time RVers choose South Dakota for the domicile for its low taxes and convenient licensing requirements. We recommend checking with AmericasMailbox.com for more information.

And watch out for firms that offer to help you establish a "limited liability corporation" to allow you to live outside the state of registry.

Many other states are chasing after their residents who form LLCs in other states — and often make their case stick with high penalties and back taxes coming due.

· · ·

Is it a good idea to rent a motorhome before buying one?

Not only is it a good idea, it's a great idea! You will learn a lot about RVing in just one short trip.

Based on what you learn, you may have a better idea of the size of a rig that will suit you and what features are important.

If you'll be traveling with a partner, you'll likely get a good idea of how well you'll get along in a tight space.

This is especially important for RVers considering taking up the full-time lifestyle. There are many places to rent a motorhome, travel trailer or truck camper.

Cruise America and El Monte RV are the best known motorhome rental companies in the USA. Peer-to-peer rental companies, operating like Airbnbs except for RVs, have become popular lately.

The best known are Outdoorsy.com and RVshare.com. Expect to pay, on average, around $80 a night for a pop-up, to as much as $200 or more a night for a Class A motorhome.

Can I park my motorhome in front of my home when I'm not traveling?

Maybe or maybe not. Many municipalities do not allow RVs on the street at all except for short periods for loading or unloading.

If you plan to buy an RV and you plan to keep it on the street or even in your driveway, be sure to check with your city or county to make sure it's okay. And even if it is legal, you might want to ask around to see if there is any talk of new laws that restrict parking an RV on private property.

.   .   .

Where else could I keep my RV if I can't keep it on the street or in my driveway?

Look for RV storage businesses in your area. They can be hard to come by, or booked solid. Also, many mini-storage businesses have space for RVs.

In a rural area you may pay $50 a month, but in or near a big city, it could be $400, $500 or more a month.

Be sure where you store your RV is secure. RVs in storage lots are common targets for thieves. Some RVers store their rigs at the homes of friends or family with extra room on their property.

A 2019 survey of RVtravel.com readers revealed that slightly more than half of the 4,800 respondents paid to store their RVs. About 20 percent of those RVers paid more than $100 a month with 1 percent paying more than $500.

Do I need to do anything to get my RV ready to store?

If you are storing over the winter, you will need to winterize the unit if you live where temperatures drop below freezing. The manufacturer will provide a set of winterizing instructions.

In general, you will have to drain all the water lines, water and waste tanks and the water heater. Some RVers add a special RV antifreeze (*do not use auto antifreeze*) and use the water pump to circulate and fill all the water lines.

In most areas of the country, humidity can be a problem. There are both electric dehumidifiers that need shore power to operate, and chemical ones that use crystals to wring moisture out of the air.

Winterizing also means removing anything unwelcome bugs or rodents might find attractive to snack on.

What's the best way to get started RVing after I buy my RV?

After you drive your new RV away, plan a two- or three-day shakedown trip close to home. Try to use all of the onboard systems on your first trip — even the air conditioner in the middle of winter to be sure it works.

Be sure to use your hookups, but it's also a good idea to spend at least one day dry camping so you can become familiar with the self-contained aspect of RVing.

Take notes on anything that doesn't work right or that you may need to consult with your dealer about. Nine out of ten RVs will have problems that need fixing, most of them easily addressed, but some serious enough to keep an RV in the repair shop for weeks — even months — on end.

2

RV DRIVING AND TOWING

Do I need a special license to drive a motorhome? In most cases, no. But if you will be driving a very large RV, check with your state's department of motor vehicles before hitting the road. Here's a website that lists state-by-state information: https://www.outdoorsy.com/blog/guide-rv-drivers-licenses-requirements

Is it hard to drive a motorhome? They look so big!

While some people are initially intimidated by the size of a motorhome, after driving one for a while they report it isn't much different than driving the family car.

Because an RV is generally larger, there are special considerations to keep in mind — like watching for overhead branches and overhangs, using mirrors more often, and making wider turns than in the family car.

A survey of RV owners by Lou Harris and Associates found that three out of four RV owners do not feel that driving or towing an RV poses any difficulty.

Experienced automobile drivers already have the basic skills to drive a motorized RV. Automatic transmissions and power brakes and steering are typical.

They seem so tall. Does that cause problems?

For most RVs most of the time, the answer is no. But for the largest Class A coaches and fifth wheel trailers, it's essential to know the total height, including roof-mounted air conditioners, so that you can avoid low clearance problems.

Drivers do need to be alert for overhead obstructions like low tree branches and drive-through awnings. A trucker's GPS can be a big help avoiding low bridges and tunnels, but a much less expensive option is to purchase Rand McNally's Motor Carriers' Atlas which lists low clearances in the USA — here's its website: https://store.randmcnally.com/motor-carriers-atlases.html

Should I sign up for an RV driving school?

Some would-be RVers find driving schools can help

them get over the intimidation of driving a large Class A motorhome or towing a trailer or fifth wheel.

Some RV dealers provide limited driving instruction, but a driving school will cover more aspects in greater depth. Classes are offered at FMCA conferences and other rallies. Do a Google search for RV driving schools.

I notice that some motorhomes do not have a back window. How do you see what is behind you?

On a smaller coach, like a 24-foot Class C, for example, the side mirrors do the job as long as you remember that you can't see someone directly behind you (like a tailgating motorcyclist).

Most large Class A motorhomes have a video camera mounted at their rear just below the roof line that sends a live picture to a monitor in the driver's compartment.

Can my family riding in the back of my motorhome move about while I'm driving down the highway?

Yes, but to minimize mishaps they should remain buckled except for brief instances. Up front in the cab, the driver and passenger will need to be belted in at all times, at least in all the states we know of. Here's a site with a state-by-state breakdown of seatbelt laws and RVers: https://www.-camperguide.org/rv-seat-belt-laws-by-state/

My kids are all excited about riding in the bed above the cab of our Class C motorhome and looking ahead out the window. Is this okay?

We do see this happening, but we do not approve. It's dangerous! Keep them below and belted into their seats.

How fast can I drive a motorhome?

If it's loaded properly and you're not headed up a steep hill, you should be able to drive the speed limit. During bad weather — heavy rains or in cross winds — slow down.

Keep in mind that it takes a lot longer to stop than with your passenger vehicle. So add extra room in front of you at all times. When winter sets in, no need to give up RVing. But remember the old trucker's admonition — it applies well to RVing: "Snow? Go slow. Ice? No go."

What's the difference between driving a motorhome and driving a car?

Generally speaking, you'll round corners slower and wider, and be more concerned about low hanging branches and roof overhangs that can do serious damage to the RV.

You'll also need to concentrate on your side mirrors more than with a car, as there is a huge "blind spot" along the right side of a rig.

And because you have lots of stuff onboard — dishes, pots and pans and other do-dads — you'll be especially interested in avoiding deep potholes and rough roads that will shake everything up. And, of course, backing up is usually more challenging.

What gas mileage should I expect with a motorhome?

A survey of 22 diesel fired motorcoach owners showed

8.1 to 8.3 mpg was average. Many of these towed a vehicle behind them. Of those surveyed, only three got better than 10 mpg, and NOBODY ever touched 11 mpg.

A gas powered coach will get less in the way of fuel economy. Some say 6 to 12 mpg, but we couldn't tie down a group of owners like we did diesel owners.

Fuel economy is a tricky subject, as there are so many variables. Uphill? Downhill? Windy conditions? "Toad" car behind you? Drive fast or slow? The figures will be all over the map. Our best advice: Plan for the worst, and be happy if you beat expectations at the fuel pump.

How about mileage towing a trailer?

In addition to the size and weight of the rig, as well as whether the tow vehicle is gas or diesel powered, your results may vary.

Factor in the same issues for motorhome economy as above, and you "might" expect 8-10 miles per gallon on gas and 10-15 on diesel. Because travel trailers have a lower wind profile, you may get slightly improved mileage versus towing a fifth wheel.

When traveling state to state in an RV, do you have to stop at truck weigh stations or have any particular papers with you?

In MOST states, no, you don't need to stop at truck scales. However, if you have a rig that scales in at more than 10,000 pounds, there are some states that do require a stop.

Here's a site that gives the details. https://camperguide. org/rvs-stop-weigh-stations/ The only papers you legally need to carry with you are the registration papers for the RV.

Of course, you must have your driver's license and proof of insurance on the vehicle you're driving.

Can I travel in Mexico and Canada with my RV?

Yes, but be sure to contact your insurance company first to be sure you are covered. In Mexico, you will need a special policy. Be sure you do this, because if you get in an accident in Mexico without the proper insurance, you can get into a lot of trouble.

For Mexico travel, your insurance must be issued by a recognized Mexican insurance company. You'll need a passport or passcard to get in and out of both Canada and Mexico. So be sure to check before starting your trip.

Unless you own your RV (and/or tow vehicle) outright, you'll need a NOTARIZED letter from the lienholder, lender, or rig owner, granting you permission to use these vehicles in Mexico.

Additionally, if you drive your RV or travel trailer beyond Mexico's "Free Zone" you'll need to purchase a Mexico Vehicle Import Permit.

The Mexico Free Zone (Liberated Zone, Perimeter Zone, or Free Trade Zone) is an area along the Mexican international land borders running inward up to the point where Mexican Customs authorities have their first "interior" check point. This is usually about 12 to 16 miles from the border towns.

There are exceptions on the peninsula of Baja, California and places like Puerto Peñasco where it runs to the ocean front along the main highways. You DON'T need this permit if you stick to driving on the Baja Peninsula or the Sonora Free Zone.

On the latter, the permit is required if you drive farther than Kilometer 98 on Mexican Federal Highway 15.

You may also be asked to have an internationally recognized credit card that bears the same name as the RV owner.

What's a toad?

This is RV jargon for the automobile that many people tow behind their motorhome for sightseeing and running errands when camped. A toad is also referred to as a "dinghy."

Can I tow my current auto behind my motorhome?

You will want to check with the manufacturer. Damage can occur if a vehicle is not approved for towing. You also don't want to void your warranty.

And remember to check your motorhome's total weight rating (Gross Combined Weight Rating, GCWR), the total weight of your loaded RV and any towed vehicle.

Finally, since most states require supplemental braking in a towed vehicle; you'll need to purchase either a portable system or have a permanent system installed. If you should get into an accident in a state where a supplemental braking system is required by law, you could get in a heap of trouble.

How much wear and tear can I expect with my toad?

You will, of course, sustain tire wear, but less than if you drove the car the same number of miles. You will want to check with the manufacturer for additional service suggestions.

Some RVers use a "dolly," a small trailer that carries the toad's front wheels. This reduces some wear on the toad.

Not all cars can be "flat towed," that is, towed with all wheels in contact with the pavement. Expensive damage can occur if you tow a car not designed for this, so always check your owner's manual before towing it.

Is it hard to hitch a toad?

No, but it's important to follow a routine so that you don't forget anything. Position your toad, hook up the tow bar, attach safety cables, then the wiring and last the break-away cable.

Make sure to check over the complete hitch setup when

you are finished. Once you do it a few times, it's fast and easy.

How is driving with a toad different?

Probably the biggest difference is that you must never back up a motorhome with a vehicle in tow four wheels down. So be extra careful about entering parking lots and campgrounds.

If you must back up for any reason, you will need to unhitch the toad first and move it out of the way. Also, with your toad hitched, your total length could be extended by 20 feet or more. You'll need to remember that when stopping or parking.

The added weight that you're towing may affect the performance of some coaches, particularly smaller ones.

I'm concerned that if I buy a fifth wheel trailer and then use the unattached pickup truck for side trips that I'll burn a lot of fuel. I'm wondering if it would be better to buy a motorhome and tow a small compact car that goes forever on a gallon of gas. What do you think?

Each way has its advantages and disadvantages. Keep in mind that with the motorhome-car combo, you'll have two engines to maintain. The extra cost might be far greater than the extra fuel you'd burn with the truck on day trips.

Our advice? Get out a calculator and figure out how many miles you're likely to drive on day trips, and then estimate the costs both ways. Add in the advantage that you can use the truck for hauling when you're not towing.

Some motorhome owners who do not tow a dinghy rent

a car at times. Enterprise can sometimes pick you up and take you to their office to complete the rental paperwork. In the long run, this can be far less expensive than owning and maintaining their own car.

I have a small truck. Can I pull a fifth wheel trailer?

Yes, a small one. Fifth wheels come in all sizes, some in short and lightweight versions that can be pulled by small trucks.

You'll need to verify that the hitch weight of the trailer when loaded does not cause the truck to exceed its Gross Vehicle Weight Rating (GVWR) and that the total weight of truck and trailer does not exceed the truck's Gross Combined Weight Rating (GCWR).

With a short bed truck you will probably need a sliding hitch. Don't forget, you'll also need a brake control installed in the truck to safely operate the trailer brakes.

Can I remove a fifth wheel hitch from my pickup when I'm not towing?

Yes. Most hitches are securely attached to rails installed in the truck bed with four pins. Remove the pins and lift out the hitch. The hitch can be heavy, so be careful.

Can I pull a travel trailer with my family car?

In many cases, yes. New lightweight towables are popular these days and can be pulled by many six-cylinder cars (and some four-cylinder ones) and sport utility vehicles.

Lightweight towables are generally less than 26 feet long

and 4,000 pounds or less with most of the features of heavier units. They typically retail for $12,000 to $26,000.

Some small folding camping trailers or teardrop-type trailers can even be pulled behind most four-cylinder cars.

I own a small SUV. Can I pull a trailer with it?

Possibly, but be careful. The length of a tow vehicle's wheelbase is very important. If it's too short for the trailer it's pulling, the driver can lose control almost instantly — very bad news.

If you question whether you can pull a particular trailer with your SUV, be sure you are absolutely certain it is up to the task by asking an expert (and not just an RV salesman, who may not be adequately informed or entirely honest).

I've heard that travel trailers can sway in windy conditions. Couldn't this be dangerous?

It can be. The good news is that equalizing hitches, also called load distributing hitches, greatly reduce sway and improve control. These are highly recommended for heavier trailers.

Another less-expensive option is installing a sway-control unit. Larger trailers will require two, but a sway-control can do much to smooth out buffeting winds, particularly when being passed by a big truck when heading downhill. But in high winds it's a good idea to slow down regardless of which type of RV or hitch you have.

I've never backed up a trailer. Is it hard to learn?

Almost anyone can learn, but it will take a little getting used to. At first it may seem like you are turning the wheel in the opposite direction from where you want to point the trailer.

Plan to take your trailer to a large empty lot and practice for a couple of hours before trying to back into any tight spots.

Are fifth wheels harder to back up?

Not harder, just a little different. The "hinge" point is a lot closer to the driver, so the response tends to be a little quicker. Again, plan on practicing for a couple of hours before you try to back it into a campsite.

What is a brake controller?

Brake controllers are smart devices that are installed on a tow vehicle to provide much improved trailer braking control. If your trailer is equipped with electric brakes (and almost all are) you'll need a brake controller to operate them.

.   .   .

Can I tow a boat or ATV trailer behind my fifth wheel or travel trailer?

This is called "triple towing" and permissibility varies from state to state. Even where allowed, there may be restrictions, so check the regulations where you plan to travel. This site provides general information for all states: https://gillettesinterstaterv.com/blog/can-you-triple-tow-an-rv-legality-and-safety.

Should I be concerned about driving steep grades in an RV?

Yes, but the key is "take it easy." Going up, this means watching your engine temperature (and transmission, too, if yours has a temperature gauge), and going down it means saving your brakes. In both cases you may need to downshift.

When descending, don't ride your brakes — use short, hard brake applications to reduce your speed by 10 miles per hour to maintain control. You should set a "maximum" speed in your mind and do the "stab and release" brake method as soon as you hit that set point.

Doesn't stuff rattle around when you are on the road in the RV?

RVers do have to take steps to deal with the consequences of the inevitable bumps and sudden stops encountered on the road.

Rubberized shelf liners help things stay put. Many folks use plastic, silicone and other non-breakable dishes and cookware. Precautions are necessary with breakables.

You'll find lots of tips on packing and stowing in RV publications and forums. Be sure before leaving for a day of travel to check drawers and cupboards to be sure they are loaded properly and their doors securely shut.

3

RV SERVICES

I carry AAA Emergency Road Service on my car. Will this also cover emergency towing on my motorhome?

No, you'll need to update to AAA Plus RV. This will cover you for up to a 100-mile tow. But coverage can be spotty in some parts of the country where you may have to arrange and pay for your own tow and then get reimbursed later.

Many RVers buy policies with other companies that specialize in RV emergency service, including the Good Sam Club, Family Motor Coach Association, Coach-Net, and others. Here are some things to consider when searching for an emergency road service plan:

• Does your plan cover all vehicles that you normally travel with: motorhome, toad, trailer?

• Does it include a lodging allowance if you aren't able to stay in your RV?

• Are you covered in Canada or Mexico? Or if you are from Canada, are you covered in the U.S.?

• Are you going to be on short trips near home or crossing the country?

• Does your plan have an upper limit? A deductible?

• What hoops do you have to jump through to get reimbursed if you have to pay cash for service?

Is there a consumer guide that rates RVs?

The RV Consumer Group, RV.org, offers this service. Some RVers claim the group has been a big help determining the quality and/or dependability of a coach.

Others say the group's reports (not cheap) were a waste of their money. Based on such varied reports we do not endorse the organization.

The best bet in determining the quality of a particular RV is to talk to people who own one, read reviews in RV magazines and on Internet forums, and then be sure to carefully inspect the unit you are interested in buying.

If you are not thoroughly experienced as an RVer, you'll be head-and-shoulders above to have a qualified RV technician inspect an RV you're interested in buying — DO NOT RELY on a seller-provided inspection.

And be sure the vehicle displays the oval-shaped seal of the Recreation Vehicle Industry Association. To qualify, a manufacturer must comply with hundreds of safety specifications that are essential for a quality unit. Be wary of any RV that does not display this seal.

4

CAMPING AND CAMPGROUNDS

I s it easy to find campgrounds?
In most cases, yes, but it's becoming increasingly difficult to find a spot easily, wiith so many new RVs being sold or rented.

It may be easier in the West than in the East because campgrounds are more plentiful in the West and there are far more public lands. But you will find campgrounds everywhere.

Altogether, there are about 16,000 private and public campgrounds in the USA. They range from primitive sites operated by the Bureau of Land Management (BLM) and U.S. Forest Service, to luxury resorts with golf courses, health clubs, swimming pools and saunas. Many websites list these campgrounds.

What do you mean by "primitive campsites?"

Primitive campsites are those with no utility hookups. There may or may not be a water spigot in the campground, and if there are toilets at all, they will usually be of the outhouse variety.

RVers in most rigs, with their onboard 12-volt electricity, generators, water tanks, waste holding tanks and bathrooms, can live comfortably in a primitive campground for a few days, and usually cheaply because primitive campsites are the least expensive places to stay short of a freebie Walmart parking lot.

And, generally speaking, primitive campsites are farther off the beaten path, thus providing peace and quiet as well as scenic beauty.

What does it mean when a campground has "full hookups"?

It means you can plug into household current electricity, fresh water, a sewer and sometimes even cable TV. When your RV is fully hooked up, you can live pretty much like at home.

Some campgrounds, especially public ones, may offer only water and electric hookups. Public campgrounds like those in state and federal parks almost never offer full hookups, but often provide water and electricity. Many also have an RV dump facility available.

How much power can I use when hooked up to electricity?

All hookups are not created equal. Public parks may offer only small amounts of power — typically 20 amps, enough to run lights, microwave, TV, a space heater, laptop computer — or a combination of a few of these at once.

The plug on these sites looks just like a plug at home. Most private RV parks provide either 30- or 50-amp service, which will adequately power air conditioners and other power-hogging devices.

The very biggest motor coaches need all the power they can get for their multiple air conditioners: A 20-amp hookup would be woefully inadequate.

What are membership campgrounds?

Membership campgrounds are for their members only. Coast-to-Coast (800-368-5721) and Thousand Trails (800-388-7788) are two examples.

The advantage to membership campgrounds is they are most often attractive and secure with plenty of activities and member interaction.

Members seldom have a problem getting a campsite; some RVers literally travel from one park to another, spending a few days or even weeks in each.

But membership campgrounds are not for everybody and unless you camp a lot are probably not cost effective.

Costs to join may run from hundreds of dollars to thousands. Most RVers do not join membership parks, camping instead at public campgrounds and private ones like KOA.

Are reservations necessary at public campgrounds?

With the huge increase of new RVers, consider a reservation a must; some popular campgrounds may not have an opening for months — even a year or more.

While "shoulder season" travel used to be a shoe-in for finding a spot, even non-summer months have become so popular that reservations are becoming mandatory.

Commercial campgrounds and public campgrounds utilizing reservations alike, get on the phone or Internet and check things out when planning your trip.

Are campgrounds safe?

Generally, yes. But there are no guarantees. Crime, alas, can occur anywhere, even in places you'd least expect it. Use common sense and you will likely never have a problem.

Our experience has been that free or very cheap campgrounds in the vicinity of major metropolitan areas would attract a higher percentage of less-than-desirable campers.

About the worst experience you will likely have in any campground is to be the unfortunate neighbor of a crowd of loud, boom-box-blasting revelers intent on polishing off a few cases of beer.

How much do campsites cost?

Forest Service campgrounds typically go for between $8 and $25, and in some places they are still free. State park campgrounds go from $15 to $45, depending on the state and location.

Private campgrounds with full hookups average from a low of $20 in out-of-the-way places to $40 to $60 in popular locations, with many $80 or more.

Be prepared to pay an additional reservation fee if you reserve a space rather than just drop in and take your chances of being turned away.

The rates at most private campgrounds, including KOA, are based on two campers per site. An additional dollar or two per extra camper may be charged as well as a fee for daily visitors.

Are discounts available?

Yes. Most RV parks offer weekly or monthly rates. Some will offer a seventh day free after paying for six days. Members of Good Sam, AAA and AARP usually qualify for discounts on daily rates, usually 10 percent.

A Passport America membership will net you 50% off at participating parks (https://passportamerica.com). At

National Park and Forest Service campgrounds, Senior Pass and Access Pass (for the disabled) holders get half off.

Do all campsites at a commercial campground cost the same?

No, a non-hookup site will be the least expensive. An option for a water and electric hookup may be offered, which will cost more. And full hookups, which include use of a sewer, go for the highest price. Some campgrounds may not offer all of these options.

An extra charge may also be levied for more than two campers in one site as well as a per-pet charge. Often more desirable sites, such as waterfront or view sites, are priced higher. In the most popular resort areas, a campsite along a beach or lake may go for $200 a night or more.

How long am I allowed to stay in a campground?

In a private RV park, often indefinitely, but at least for a season. But in public campgrounds, like those in state and federal parks, stays may be limited to one to two weeks.

Stays of up to seven months are allowed on some public lands in the Southwest; more about that later.

What are the advantages and disadvantages of a private campground over a public one?

Each has its pluses and minuses, and it's difficult to generalize. However, the plus side to a private campground (usually) is that full hookups are available (electric, water and sewer), and it's likely that other amenities will be available like Wi-Fi, laundry, playgrounds, swimming pool, TV lounge, propane, and a small general store.

Private campgrounds also tend to be located closer to towns and/or tourist areas. Public campgrounds, on the other hand, like those in state and national parks and national forests, are more often in scenic or recreational areas, and campsites may be larger and more private.

These are just generalizations. Individual parks, private and public, vary hugely in appearance, location and amenities.

What's the difference between a campground and an RV park?

Public facilities like those found on government lands are almost always called campgrounds. Privately owned campgrounds are usually called RV parks, but not always.

RV parks that cater to luxury RVs are often called RV resorts, although the term is often used by less-than-luxurious parks to spiff up their image.

I camp a lot. Do you have any tips about how I can save money at private campgrounds?

Two ways come to mind. Join the Good Sam Club. As a member, you will receive an automatic 10 percent savings at most private campgrounds.

You can also purchase a KOA Value Kard for $33 at any KOA campground, or on its website. The card entitles you to a 10 percent discount at all of the hundreds of KOAs in North America.

Perhaps the best way to save money at campgrounds is to stay in non-hookup sites, where the cost will likely be 20 to 25% less than with a full-hookup site.

Passport America offers an annual membership for $44 that permits half-price stays at about 1,600 commercial campgrounds. This is an excellent deal for RVers who travel a lot. Also check out the popular Escapees RV Club.

Do I need a membership to camp at KOA?

No, no membership is required. But if you purchase an annual KOA Value Card for $33, you'll receive 10 percent off the price of a campsite when you stay.

I have heard that some campgrounds will not allow RVs older than ten years to stay there. Is this true?

Yes, particularly in high-end RV resorts that cater to well-to-do RVers in expensive rigs. The park is trying to prevent old, beat up RVs from trashing its appearance.

Some parks will ask you to send a photo of your older RV before letting you make a reservation. The solution is to drive something that isn't old and ugly or simply avoid such parks.

. . .

Is it true that some RV parks do not allow children?

It's only true in some regions popular with retirees, usually "snowbird" RV parks where older folks head for the winter.

A few of these private "senior-only" parks (most of them located in Arizona or Florida) will even deny camping to anyone under 55 (with exceptions). But all public campgrounds allow people of every age, as do perhaps 99 percent of all private RV parks.

Are pets allowed in campgrounds?

Yes, almost always. Some parks may have a limit of how many pets, with an extra charge per pet, even the first one. It's usually only a couple of dollars, but we've seen it as high as $10. So be sure to ask about extra charges for pets before making a reservation.

If you have a large dog or one that is perceived as an "aggressive breed," always check when making a reservation. Sometimes the dog will not be allowed, usually because of insurance restrictions.

Is it okay to smoke in campgrounds?

While at least a few local governments have banned outdoor smoking, none have made this apply to RV parks.

Some private RV parks have banned smoking, or limited it to specific areas in their parks. If you're concerned, call in advance.

What about alcohol?

Some RV parks post signs against alcohol in their park.

Does that mean consumption is prohibited outside your RV? Pretty likely.

How about in the privacy of the inside of your rig? Some think not, but we know of at least one RV park that prohibits alcohol on their grounds.

Check the park rules (many have them on their website) and if it's not clear, call in advance. And remember, possession of alcohol on many tribal reservations is completely verboten.

What are check-in and check-out times at campgrounds?

In many cases, check-in time is 2 p.m. or 3 p.m. Most RV parks request you leave by 11 a.m., but many others allow you to stay until noon or even 1 p.m., which we hope will become a trend.

We plan to camp a lot in National Forests. What length RV will fit in their campsites?

National Forests vary greatly in the size of RVs they will accommodate. A small percentage will accommodate the largest rigs, but many will not accommodate a long trailer or fifth wheel with their tow vehicles, or even a 40-foot motorhome.

We're guessing now, but based on years of camping in National Forest campgrounds we'd estimate small- to medium-sized trailers and fifth wheels will fit in about two-thirds of USFS campgrounds.

Motorhomes 28 feet or shorter will probably fit with no problems. Don't ignore length warnings — the photos you may see posted may look like they'll accommodate your rig, but tight turns in campground roads may completely put your rig out of the running.

How do you level an RV when a campsite is not level?

Most mid- to high-end motorhomes have leveling systems — some fully automatic. With less expensive units and trailers, wooden planks or plastic leveling blocks under a tire or two will do the job.

Leveling is a critical matter. Many RV refrigerators, for example, can be permanently damaged when operated too far off-level.

Aren't most campsites level?

No. In private parks, perhaps two-thirds are level or close to level. But in public campgrounds, especially those in National Forests, most campsites will require you to level up. It's not uncommon to find campsites that are so out of whack that getting level is nearly impossible.

What are the best guides to campgrounds?

The only major directory still published is from the Good Sam Club. It's primarily a guide to commercial RV parks rather than public campgrounds. It's available at Camping World and most RV dealer stores.

KOA publishes a free annual directory of its campgrounds that also includes a good road atlas of the USA and Canada. There is a plethora of information on campgrounds and other camping areas on the Internet, and there are several fine campground apps available for tablets and smartphones, both Android and Apple.

Do campgrounds have restrooms with showers?

Nearly all private campgrounds (RV parks) and many state and national parks have these facilities, but other public campgrounds may not.

All but the most primitive have toilets, although in some cases this might mean an old-fashioned outhouse.

Can I pick my own campsite at a campground or is it picked for me?

In most public campgrounds you select your own spot. But in perhaps half of private campgrounds, the site will be assigned to you when you arrive. If you don't like it, you can request another one, space permitting.

What about spending the night at rest areas?

Overnighting at a rest stop in your RV is legal in many states, even those with posted "no camping" signs.

There's a difference between putting up a tent, or putting out slideouts (generally viewed as camping), and taking a night's rest unobtrusively. Check this website out for state-specific information: https://www.interstaterestareas.com/overnight-parking-rules/.

Observe common-sense safety precautions: Don't open your door to anyone at night. If it feels "wrong," then move along. Be prepared for an uncomfortable night, with plenty of traffic noise. Don't put out chairs or barbecues.

I've heard you can stay the night in Walmart parking lots and similar places. Is this true?

Yes, this is generally true. Many Walmarts across the USA will permit an overnight stay in a self-contained RV.

But always look for "No overnight parking" signs in the parking lot before you put on your pajamas. And, no, it is **not** OK to stay in a pop-up trailer (although we have seen it done).

The idea is to blend in to the surroundings — to be invisible. Here are some tips for proper Walmart etiquette:

- You should ask permission to stay.
- Park in a corner of the lot, away from shoppers.
- Do not extend your slideouts unless absolutely necessary.
- Do not extend your awning.
- Do not put down automatic levelers as they can damage the pavement.
- Keep your lawn chairs, grills, and any other belongings inside or in storage.

Walmart is not a campground. Stay a night to get some sleep, shop in the store to say "thank you" and then move on. Do not abuse this privilege.

I see a sign in many parking lots that says "RV Parking." Does this mean I can stay the night?

Probably not. It simply identifies the area where RVs should be parked. When you see "RV parking" advertised on billboards, it usually means that there is plenty of space to park an RV if you choose to visit. It does not mean you can stay the night, although sometimes that's true.

What are "pull-thru" campsites?

These are campsites where you can drive in to the site and then drive the same direction going out. They are very handy for RVers with long trailers, fifth wheels or motorhomes pulling a car because the RV will enter and exit the space without needing to back up. For a short stay, there is no need to even unhook the towed vehicle.

Do campgrounds have stores to buy groceries, fishing tackle — things like that?

Some do, including all KOA campgrounds, which sell

basic groceries, RV supplies, souvenir items and even rent DVDs. Other private campgrounds may have similar stores.

But public campgrounds, like those in state and federal parks, seldom have stores, although sometimes there's one just down the road.

I need to get online. Do campgrounds offer Wi-Fi service?

Increasingly, yes. But if you really, really need to get online, don't depend on the campground's Wi-Fi service. It is often unavailable or painfully slow because too many other RVers are hogging the limited bandwidth by watching videos.

Sometimes, the Wi-Fi system itself may not reach the entire park. Some parks will charge for a faster service. If you want to be sure the Wi-Fi is adequate for your needs, call the park.

It's not a bad idea to drive through the park before selecting a site, if allowed, as the Wi-Fi may be excellent in one area but weak or nonexistent in others.

How else can I get Internet access away from public Wi-Fi?

Check with your wireless phone provider (Verizon, AT&T, T-Mobile, etc.). You may be able to use your cell phone as a Wi-Fi hotspot.

Better yet, buy a Mi-Fi device that can be connected to a cellular network to provide internet access for five to ten devices. Our experience is that Verizon has the most reliable coverage, including in rural areas.

.   .   .

What does the term "boondocking" mean?

It means camping outside a campground, usually for free, and relying on onboard water supplies and 12-volt DC power systems.

Many RVers boondock for weeks and even months on end during the winter on public lands in the Southwest. They charge their rigs' deep cycle batteries with solar panels or by cranking up the generator now and then.

By conserving water and liquid waste, they can minimize trips to the dump stations. In some popular desert boondocking spots, a "honey wagon" will come by to empty the waste tanks for a reasonable fee.

OK, then what is dry camping?

Some RVers use the terms boondocking and dry camping interchangeably, while others distinguish dry camping as any time you spend the night without hookups, and boondocking as dry camping in the "boonies," i.e., away from campgrounds, parking lots and rest areas.

What is pavement camping?

It's when you park your RV for the night on pavement, like in a store parking lot or along the curb on a quiet street. Parking in a hospital or church parking lot would also be considered pavement parking.

I like the idea of boondocking but I wonder how I would get along without being able to plug in my electrical appliances.

A generator, of course, will allow you to use all the electrical appliances you'd use at home.

A very inexpensive alternative, however, is to buy a small power inverter, which plugs into a 12-volt socket (cigarette lighter) and will convert your onboard 12-volt power into household current.

You won't be able to run major appliances with a small inverter, but they provide enough juice for TVs, VCRs, battery chargers, computers and other low-power devices. You can buy these at Walmart and Amazon for $35 and up.

Serious boondockers outfit their RVs with solar panels, additional deep cycle batteries and more powerful, permanently installed inverters.

If they watch their power usage (as well as water) they can stay in one place for weeks at a time without ever hooking up. Of course, in the dead of winter when the sun doesn't shine much, they won't have much power to work with.

How long can I boondock at one time?

There's no short answer here. It depends on the fresh- and waste-water capacity of your rig, your battery capacity and whether you have a generator or solar panels, how many people are camping, and how good you are at conserving water and power.

If you can bring in additional fresh water and haul away your waste to a dump site, then you may be able to extend your stay nearly indefinitely.

What's stealth camping?

This is a recent term which applies to people who travel

or even live in vans, usually without windows behind the driver's compartment.

The idea is you don't want to draw attention to yourself when stealth camping, so you try to park where you blend in with every other parked vehicle.

If the vans do have windows, the occupants may use blackout curtains so they don't draw attention to themselves.

Many stealth campers choose this way to travel, or even live, out of economic necessity. Others are simply minimalists who prefer to live as simply as possible.

We plan to travel by motorhome but we won't pull a car. This will limit our traveling in the evening after we pull into a campground. Will we get bored?

Your options after settling in for the night are far more limited without a car than with one. That's pretty obvious.

There are a few tricks, though. First, try to find campgrounds that are within walking distance of places where there's something to do — a store, restaurant, small town main street or even a lake where you can fish or swim or hike. Use Google Maps or Google Earth to identify these places.

A very good idea is to bring along bicycles, which will vastly expand the area you can explore. If you don't have room for a bike rack, buy folding bicycles.

For even more mobility, bring along a small, lightweight motorcycle or scooter. Have you seen the new electric bicycles on the market? They're not much heavier than a regular bicycle, but can move along effortlessly at about 15 miles per hour. Or you can pedal them if you want to extend their range and get some exercise, too.

But the real answer to your question is that you will likely find many things to do right in your campground, including just plain relaxing. Read a book, sew, draw, putter around the rig, watch TV, write letters, listen to music, sit by the fire, visit with other campers, email and surf the web if you have Internet access, etc. The list is endless.

Where can I camp for free?

You can camp for up to two weeks at no charge on U.S. government land (BLM or National Forest) unless camping is specifically prohibited.

After the two weeks, you'll need to move to another location, where you can spend another two weeks for free. In the Southwest deserts, an option is to pay $180 to stay up to seven months in a Long-Term Visitation Area (LTVA).

Several LTVAs are located in Arizona and Southern California. Many have primitive toilets (few and far between), sewage dump facilities and dumpsters. Some are even serviced by water trucks and a "honey wagon," which, for a modest fee, will drive right up to your RV and pump out your waste tanks.

RVers on a very, very tight budget find many ways to

camp elsewhere for free — holing up in discount store and casino parking lots, roadside rests, truck stops, or anywhere else they figure they won't be bothered.

Most Walmarts will allow overnight stays in their parking lots. While it's possible to "camp" like this forever, most RVers find the hassle too much trouble, at least on a regular basis.

What's a Snowbird?

An RVer who follows the sun. In the West that means heading to the Southwest when it gets cold and rainy in the North. In the East, it means heading to Florida. In the Midwest, it probably means heading to the Gulf Coast. Some RVers even venture into Mexico.

5

RV SYSTEMS

Does it matter what order I hook up water, electrical and sewer?

Not technically, but it's a good idea to start with the electrical hookup while your hands are dry. Then hook up the fresh water while your hands are clean. Finally, hook up the sewer lines and then wash up.

How do I plug my RV into the power pedestal?

First, you will have three choices of plugs, 20 amp (looks like your wall outlet at home), 30 amp and 50 amp. Few RVers can get by with 20 amps: it's not enough power to run much more than lights, a TV and a few other low-energy appliances.

Most of the RVs on the market today are wired for 30-amp and 50-amp service. You can easily tell by the plug. Be sure to turn the breaker switch off before plugging in or unplugging your RV. Once plugged in, flip the switch.

My RV is rated for 50 amps. Can I plug it into a 30-amp hookup at a campground?

Yes, you can. Get a quality dog-bone adapter (see below) from a respected company such as Camco. The one you want has a 30-amp male connector on one end and a 50-amp female connector on the other.

But realize that while a 50-amp outlet can provide a total of 12,000 watts of power, a 30-amp outlet can only provide 3,600 watts of power maximum. So you won't be able to run everything at once in your RV without tripping a circuit breaker at the pedestal.

What's a dogbone adapter?

It's an electrical adapter with a pair of power connectors separated by a foot-or-so-long piece of heavy black wire. They allow you to connect a 50-amp shore power cord from your RV to a 30- or even 15-amp electrical outlet, or visa versa. They sort of look like a cartoon version of a bone that a dog carries in his mouth, hence the name "dogbone."

I hear it's important to have a surge protector to protect my RV from damage

It's important to have a surge protector to protect your RV from damage, but be aware that not all surge protectors are created equal. You really want one that has a built-in EMS function (Electrical Management System) with a relay that can disconnect your RV from dangerous power situations. Expect to pay around $250 to $400 for an EMS surge protector.

The inexpensive $100 (or less) models only deal with electrical spikes (from, for example, nearby lightning strikes) but won't turn off power to your RV if the pedestal voltage gets too high, too low, or the ground is lost.

Surge Guard and Progressive Industries both make EMS surge protectors that will help keep you and your RV safe from electrical harm.

.   .   .

What do I do about power when my RV is not plugged into an electric outlet?

Your RV's 12-volt electrical system (powers lights, water pump, fans, etc.) takes care of most things you need. Most RV refrigerators run on LP gas.

Without shore power from an electrical hookup you'll be without your air conditioner, microwave oven and television. A small electrical device called an inverter can change your 12-volt RV power into something a laptop computer or other low-power devices need.

If your shore power-hungry devices need 300 watts or less, a suitable inverter can be had for less than $50. At that amount of power, these inverters will need to be connected directly to your RV battery with what looks like jumper cable clamps.

It's best to purchase a "pure sine wave" inverter, as the power they provide can be used by most any device, provided you don't exceed the power output.

Larger inverters can be wired into your RV and will support bigger devices, but require more expertise than we can include here.

I keep running across warnings about RV "hot-skin conditions." What does that mean?

A hot-skin condition is extremely dangerous. It's when the skin (and chassis, hitch, wheels, etc.) of your RV develops more than 2 or 3 volts above the earth (ground) below it. Any hot skin over 40 volts AC can be lethal under the right conditions.

· · ·

Is it normal to feel a little tingle when I touch my RV's front door to open it?

NO! NEVER! NYET! If your RV is properly grounded from the shore power connection, it should never be more than 2 or 3 volts above earth ground.

If you can feel a tingle, you likely have at least 20 volts of hot-skin voltage. That means you've lost the electrical ground on your RV and it can develop lethal voltages (up to 120 volts) at any time.

Any tingle is a warning to immediately unplug from shore power and get the wiring fixed before someone gets hurt or killed. For a complete discussion of hot skin conditions and how to protect yourself, go to www.rvtravel.com and search for how to test for a hot skin on your RV.

I plan to keep my RV at home, but will need a long extension to reach an outlet. Is this okay?

Yes, but the extension cord must be rated to carry the maximum amperage that your home outlet can deliver. Be aware that even a 15-amp "Edison" outlet will likely be powered by a 20-amp circuit breaker, so you'll want to use a 12-gauge extension cord that's rated for 20 amps.

Do not use skinny orange extension cords. And never, ever use an extension cord like you'd commonly use at home to run things like floor lamps.

Is an RV protected from being hit by lightning?

It can be, but not always. While you, yourself, will probably survive a direct lightning hit while sitting inside of a metal (aluminum) RV, fiberglass and canvas RVs don't offer this type of protection. And a direct lightning strike on your RV will probably blow out all of the electrical systems.

Even a nearby lightning ground strike can travel up your shore power cord, blow up your surge protector or EMS, and destroy your RV's internal wiring. It's best practice to unplug your RV from pedestal power and seek shelter in a large building during severe electrical storms.

I see RVs with solar panels. Are they a good idea?

These RVers probably boondock or dry camp a lot — that is, stay in places without power for long stretches. You see this a lot in the winter in the Arizona desert.

With solar panels, RVers can keep their rigs' batteries charged or, at the very least, slow their discharge. Solar power has its limitations depending on factors such as time of year, weather, amount of tree cover and region of the country. But the answer for most RVers is "yes."

Some are able to provide nearly all their electrical power needs from photo-voltaic solar panels mounted on the RV roof and stored in a bank of deep cycle batteries. For others it reduces the time they need to run their generators when dry camping, saving fuel and eliminating noise and exhaust fumes.

Is it worth it to upgrade an RV's interior lights to LEDs?

Yes, because LED bulbs draw less than 10% of the power that an equivalent tungsten bulb needs for the same amount of light. That means LED bulbs will run 10 times as long as regular (tungsten) bulbs on the same amount of battery power.

Will the plugs in my RV work if I am not hooked up to electricity?

It depends. If you are running from a generator, typically all of your 120-volt outlets will work, but you might only be able to start up one air conditioner before tripping the circuit breaker on the generator.

If you have an inverter, it will convert the 12 volts of your battery into 120-volts AC to run some appliances. But your power will be limited to low-power appliances, so in most cases the inverter will only run your television and a few other low-power appliances.

If you only have a house battery and a converter, none of your 120-volt outlets will work at all. But the battery will supply 12-volts DC power for all RV lighting, and in some cases your television and USB charging outlets.

Can I blow a fuse in my RV like at home?

Yes, fuses are generally used on the 12-volt DC side of your power panel, while circuit breakers are always used for the 120-volt AC power side. So be sure you know the location of your fuse box and to pack extra fuses. Learn how to replace a fuse or reset a circuit breaker in case a fuse blows or a circuit breaker trips.

Tell me more about power inverters.

Power inverters are devices that convert 12-volt DC power to 120-volt household current, enabling you to power many appliances and devices.

Small inverters plug into a cigarette lighter and have a regular 120-volt outlet on the other end which you can use to power a computer, television or stereo.

Larger, costlier inverters are normally permanently installed in RVs, and in combination with a few deep cycle batteries can power high-energy appliances like microwaves.

A small power inverter is very useful for charging batteries of digital cameras, computers and smartphones. Some RVers carry a small, plug-inverter for this reason alone, charging batteries as they roll down the road.

What's the difference between an RV power converter and power inverter?

A power "converter" converts the 120-volt AC power

from a campground pedestal or generator into 12-volt DC power for charging your RV's house batteries as well as running all your 12-volt electrical appliances such as your water pump, lights, etc.

An "inverter" inverts the 12-volts DC from your battery back into 120-volt AC power that can run bigger appliances, such as your microwave oven or refrigerator. That allows you to run these larger appliances (though typically for a pretty short time) from your RV's house batteries, even when you're not plugged into a campground pedestal outlet or running from a generator.

What is a deep cycle battery?

Also called a house battery, it's used exclusively for the living area of an RV, and not to start the vehicle.

The engine battery is designed only for short, high-current use to start the engine. The house battery, on the other hand, is designed for long, low-current use, and it prefers to be charged slowly and carefully.

Most RVs have more than one deep cycle battery. The more batteries, the longer your onboard power will last before you need to recharge it. The batteries are charged in several ways: as you drive, when you are hooked up to 120-volt power, by a generator and/or by solar power.

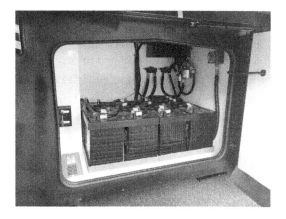

Speaking of draining a deep cycle battery, what if I do, somehow, drain my deep cycle batteries? How will I start my motorhome's engine?

The motorhome's engine has a separate battery that is only used for its automotive functions, including starting the engine. So even if you totally drain your "house" batteries, the engine will start normally and will then begin charging the drained deep cycle batteries.

If you have a generator, you can charge the deep cycle batteries using it, too. But be sure to carry battery cables with you just in case you somehow drain the battery of the motorhome's engine, or if it suddenly goes bad. The RVer in the next campsite will usually be happy to provide his or her battery for a jump.

Some motorhomes have what are variously called a boost switch or auxiliary start switch. It kicks a relay that temporarily ties the house batteries to the engine battery — kind of like jump starting — allowing you to start up the engine without jumper cables. But you need to check your owner's manual for location and how to use it.

. . .

What is shore power?

The word "shore power" comes from the marine industry where your boat was plugged into an outlet on the dock. For RVs it's a power cord that's plugged into an electrical outlet at a campground (the pedestal) or home (your garage or exterior outlet).

You can run on 20-, 30- or 50-amp shore power or your house batteries (which could also be charged from solar panels), or a built-in or portable generator.

What are my choices for "house" batteries?

The three types are:

1. Flooded cell (traditional lead-acid) that require proper venting, and checking water levels

2. AGM (Absorbed Glass Matt), which don't require checking or adding water

3. Lithium Iron-Oxide, which have the highest power density and longest charge/recharge life of the three technologies

The three types are not interchangeable, nor can they be connected together.

.   .   .

Are lithium batteries worth their high cost?

It may not make economic sense if you're only an occasional RVer who can easily run on the original battery supplied by the manufacturer.

If you want to boondock (camp without electrical or sewer hookups) for extended times and avoid running out of battery power, then Lithium batteries could be a cost-effective solution when you also factor in their extended charge/recharge cycles compared to traditional flooded cell batteries.

Why would I want to equip my RV with a generator?

To use it to power an air conditioner, microwave, electric heater or other major power-eaters and to charge your automotive and deep cycle batteries when you are dry camping (camping without utility hookups).

Is a generator really necessary?

No. If you don't have big power needs while boondocking, then you don't need a generator. If you never use it or seldom use it, you're just carrying along extra weight and using space that could be used for storage.

If you're financing an RV that came equipped with a generator, over time it will cost you a lot more than its sticker price when interest rates are figured in.

If you ever decide you need a generator you can have one installed at any time. Some people simply buy a small portable generator like those made by Honda and Yamaha.

How do I put fresh water in my RV?

There are two ways. To fill your freshwater storage tank, first hook up a hose to a water faucet. Insert the male end of the hose into the opening in the fresh water fill-up area on the side of the rig. Turn on the hose and let 'er go until the tank begins to overflow, then turn off the water.

On some RVs, you'll hook the "male" end of the hose to a special fitting, then turn a lever to direct water into the tank. You'll know when the tank is full when water shoots out of a fitting underneath your rig.

In either event, this water will later be pumped by the water pump from an onboard tank to your faucet, shower or toilet during those times when you are unable to hook up directly to a water faucet.

When you are able to hook up, attach the male end of the hose to the RV and the other to the campground faucet, then turn on the water and keep it on. The water will bypass the storage tank and feed right to the RV's faucets, etc.

When you are hooked up like this with the sewer hose hooked up you can run water just like at home without worrying about draining your water supply or filling up your waste water holding tanks.

Many RVers suggest you **do not** leave your gray (sink and shower) water valves open, but leave them closed and empty the tank when it's nearly full.

And *never* leave the black (toilet) water valve open. Let the tank fill to at least 2/3rds capacity, then dump it. It's a good idea to filter all the water that goes into your RV. Inline filters are available at most RV supply stores.

Will a regular garden hose work to fill my RV's tank?

Never fill your tank with a garden hose. They aren't designed for potable water, and in addition to possibly having mold and an off-taste, they may leach chemicals (including lead) into your tank. You certainly don't want to drink that! Buy and use only hoses that are drinking water (potable) rated.

Should I turn on the campground's water faucet all the way?

Most of the time, it's fine. If the water pressure is high — and at many campgrounds a sign will warn so — make sure to put a pressure regulator on the hose.

These inexpensive devices will prevent the high water pressure from damaging or even destroying your RV's water system. It's a good idea to use a regulator all the time. It can't hurt, and may save you a lot of inconvenience and expense.

When you use a pressure regulator, put it between the campground faucet and your RV water hose. That way, the regulator will protect both RV *and* hose.

Some RVers complain that a regulator reduces the water pressure so much it's nearly impossible to take a shower.

Spending a few extra dollars on an adjustable water pressure regulator can alleviate that problem.

Where can I fill up with fresh water when I'm not able to hook up?

First of all, plan ahead. If you think you'll be in the boondocks and far from an easy water source, then fill up whenever the opportunity presents itself and be extra careful about water use. And when you run low, just keep an eye open as you head down the road. Most rest areas with a dump station will also have a fresh water spigot.

When you fill up at a gas station, ask the attendant if you can fill up with water, too. We've filled up at all kinds of places through the years — city parks, schools, businesses where a faucet was handy (after asking the store manager if it's okay), picnic grounds, churches, etc.

Ask permission if you think it's necessary, especially if you suspect the water you use is charged to its owner by volume and not a flat fee — in which case we would offer to pay a dollar or two. This is hardly ever necessary, though. Some RVers carry filled five-gallon plastic water jugs for when their regular tank runs low.

How do I use the RV's water pump?

Simple. Flip a switch. It should be very visible inside the RV, usually in the bathroom or on a control panel with other gauges that show water tank levels and battery condition.

Be sure to turn off the water pump when it's not needed and when traveling. You do not need to use the pump when you are hooked up to a water source (faucet).

·　·　·

Speaking of gauges, are they dependable?

Good question. Alas, according to a poll of 3,200 RVtravel.com readers, less than 12 percent said their gauges were "very accurate." Another 49 percent said they were not generally accurate and 40 percent reported they were not accurate.

Sometimes my water pump goes on, then turns right off. Is that normal?

If you've just used water, it's not uncommon. But if you are not using any water, the pump should remain silent. A pump that "bumps" when there is no demand for water (open faucet tap or toilet being flushed) indicates a waterline leak in your rig.

Turn off the pump immediately to prevent more leakage, then track down and repair the leak. Water leaks can literally destroy your RV.

Where is the propane tank located on an RV and how and where do you fill up?

The propane will be in its own compartment accessible from the outside of the RV. On many travel trailers it will be right up front; fifth wheel trailers will usually have them up-front, but in a compartment.

Motorhomes have permanently mounted units, often out of sight, but with a filler connection behind a door. Propane is most readily available at commercial campgrounds and gas stations. Prices vary, but usually it costs less per gallon than gasoline. There is never self-service on propane.

How long will a tank of propane last?

How much propane used varies widely among RVers. Furnaces or LP-fired heaters chew up gas at a famous rate. Water heaters use plenty of LP, so how often do you shower?

Perhaps the smallest gas user is your refrigerator, but the hotter the weather, the more gas it will use. Many motorhomes have a gauge that will help you determine how much gas is left in the tank.

Trailer users don't usually have that luxury, so when you see the indicator flag on the propane regulator change color, know that it's time to fill one cylinder.

How will I know if my propane tank is leaking?

Most newer RVs are equipped with a propane detector that will alert you loud and clear if you have propane in your air. Otherwise, your first indicator will probably be the smell of rotten eggs. This smell is added to propane to alert you to leaks.

If you smell propane in your RV, open windows and get outside immediately and turn off the tank. Have your RV checked before turning it back on. If there is a leak, it will most often be a minor repair.

How do RV toilets work?

They look much like a toilet at home except they use hardly any water. After use, you pull a handle or press a lever and a drain opens to allow the waste to fall into the holding tank while water swirls around to help the process.

We prefer toilets where, when you flush, the tank empties into the tank directly below the toilet. On some fifth wheels, the pipes may take a right or left turn on their way to the tank. Some RVers report problems with this setup.

Do I need special toilet paper?

No, unless you want to toss away your money. You can buy special biodegradable toilet paper in RV supply stores, but it costs double or triple the price of regular toilet paper.

Most brands of plain, white, single-ply paper will decompose fine and save you money. Costco's Kirkland brand toilet paper is a good choice.

Never put Kleenex, wipes or anything else down your tank even if it says septic safe — just toilet paper.

Do I need to put chemicals in my toilet?

According to an RVtravel.com survey, about 90 percent of RVers use some kind of additive, which helps to break down solid material and prevent odors. Check with your local RV supply store.

There are many brands of chemicals available. Choose one that is environmentally friendly. If you are concerned about odors from your tank, install a 360 Siphon Vent on your roof vent. It will draw odors out of your tank.

The cheap vent covers installed by manufacturers force stinky gasses into your rig, not out.

How do you dump an RV's waste tanks?

"Dump stations" are located in most private campgrounds, in many public campgrounds, and at some gas stations and highway rest areas. Some are free but $5 to $10 per use is becoming the norm.

The process is so easy that you seldom even get your hands wet, and then usually only from the water faucet when rinsing off the sewer hose.

But how do I actually dump the tanks?

First, put on disposable gloves to protect your health. Then hook up the flexible sewer hose and insert the other end into the dump drain.

Remember to dump the black water (toilet) tank first by pulling its handle, usually attached to a 3" plastic pipe, located low on the rig on the driver side.

After it's dumped and flushed, dump the gray water tank, the one that holds the sink and shower water. These gray water lines are often fitted to a smaller 2" plastic pipe.

The gray water will wash out wastes from the black tank, making it more pleasant to wash off your sewer hose afterwards. If you do it in reverse order, put a clothespin on your nose.

Is dumping the holding tanks a disgusting job?

No. If you know what you're doing, it's easy and not an unpleasant chore. The waste passes from the RV down into the sewer effortlessly without any spillage or odor.

Of course, that's if you do things right. Be aware that the cheapest sewer hoses (usually brown) may develop pinhole leaks after minimal use.

It pays to get a higher quality hose. Drain Master has excellent products, and at least one RVtravel.com staffer has had excellent results with RhinoFLEX hoses.

Should I wear gloves while dumping the holding tanks?

When we surveyed RVers on this question, about three-quarters reported that they did, indeed, wear gloves while dumping, which you should do.

If not and you have an open cut on your hand, if bacteria should enter it you could end up in a bad way. Disposable gloves are best. P

lease *don't* leave your "used" gloves lying around at the dump station — throw them away in an appropriate trash can or take them with you for disposal.

. . .

What do I do with the sewer hose when it's not in use?

In most Class A motorhomes, the hose will store right inside the compartment where it is used. Many RVs have tubular rear bumpers that accommodate the hose.

Some RVers attach a section of four-inch plastic pipe beneath their rigs for storing their hose. By all means, keep it as far from your fresh water hose as possible.

Is it okay to just pull off in the middle of nowhere to dump the holding tanks?

No. Never! Just think if everybody did this! The country-side would be polluted and it would stink! Don't ever do this! Only dump in approved places.

If you park your RV at your home, it's probably okay to use your gray water to water plants if you use earth-friendly soaps and shampoos. But never do it in public places.

When I am hooked up to a sewer in a campground should I open both holding tanks?

No. Keep both closed. The gray water (sink and shower) will evacuate the tank more efficiently if the tank has some volume when emptied, so best to leave the tank closed until it's almost filled up.

Always (always, always) keep water in the black water tank (a gallon or two) so the additives can do their work to break up the solids. Opening the black water tank when hooked up will enable solids, including paper, to rest on the bottom and build up, and in the process create a "poop mountain" and a major stink!

It's wise to research the proper use of holding tanks to be sure they work properly and don't end up making your rig smell like a pit toilet.

I've noticed that most commercial campgrounds that offer full hookups, including sewer, also have a dump station. Why would they have a dump station if the campsites have their own sewer connection? Do you have to dump the toilet water in one place and the dish and shower water at the other?

No. They offer sewer hookups, plus provide a dump station for RVers who do not choose full-hookup campsites. These RVers may need to dump their holding tanks when arriving and/or when departing the campground, hence the need for a dump station.

Also, some RV parks earn extra income by charging a small fee for RVers who need to dump but don't stay the night.

Both the gray water and black water tanks can be emptied into either the campsite's sewer connection or at the dump station.

6

RV LIVING

My wife and I are considering buying a Class C motorhome but are concerned about getting in and out of the cab-over bunk. What do you think?

If you are not physically fit or suffer from achy bones, these bunks can be a true inconvenience. Although the beds are typically queen-sized (generally smaller than "residential queens"), one person will be pinned against the front of the rig, so getting up at night to use the bathroom means doing a sort of "push up" over their partner.

Also, making one of these beds is challenging. They're great for younger RVers who are physically active, and for kids. But older RVers should try a test run on this type of bed while at the RV dealership (or by renting an RV for a short trip) before they commit to sleeping on one for days or weeks on end.

What kitchen appliances come with RVs?

Most everything you have at home. Microwaves come in all but the least expensive units, and many RV kitchens even include built-in coffee makers.

RVs come fully furnished with furniture and appliances that include stove, oven, refrigerator and kitchen sink. Unlike a regular home, where you have to buy furnishings and appliances, an RV is basically ready to live in.

How does an RV camping vacation cost compare with one taken by car?

The RV Industry Association, whose mission is to promote RVing, preaches over and over that traveling with an RV is the cheapest way to travel.

But it's not necessarily true. If an RV is only used a month or two in a year, then the year-long cost of owning the RV including insurance, registration fees, maintenance and its depreciation needs to be figured in.

In that case, RVing is seldom the cheapest way to travel, and often far more expensive. If it's used much of the year, then, absolutely, it can definitely be more affordable per day of use than staying in hotels and dining out all the time. But, really, who ever does that?

I am on a very tight budget. Does this mean RVing is not for me?

Not necessarily. If you purchase an inexpensive RV that's in good shape, and are able to do much of the maintenance yourself, the cost of traveling by RV can be very low.

Some folks manage to do it on their income from Social Security by limiting their driving and by camping on public lands or in campgrounds that offer low monthly or seasonal rates.

Some RVers are able to avoid paying any camping fees by boondocking or spending nights in places like Walmart parking lots, where the stay is free.

What unusual amenities might I find in an RV?

Believe it or not, we once came across a couple who had installed a waterbed in their motorhome. A laundry chute to a basement laundry compartment is found in some RVs.

Electric faux-fireplaces are available in many RVs these days. Washers and dryers are built into some of the large RVs.

Dishwashers, built-in vacuums, full-size bathtubs, heated floors, wine coolers and even hide-away pet bowls are also found.

We saw a motorhome once at an RV show that had a staircase leading to the roof where there was a deck for lounging or for viewing a sporting event high above the crowds. We also know of an RV with a propeller: It can be driven right into a lake and used as a houseboat.

. . .

Do RVs have both hot and cold water?

Yes. Virtually all RVs have a water heater (six gallons is most common), powered by propane or electricity (flip a switch to choose). On gas the water will heat up in about 15 minutes and provide an adequate shower.

How do you take a shower in an RV?

If you are relying on your onboard water supply and waste water tanks, generally you'll have to be a water miser. However, if your rig is fully hooked up to water and sewer you can shower just like at home.

When "boondocking" or camping without water hookups, RVers generally take a "Navy" shower — first getting themselves wet, then soaping with the water turned off, and then rinsing. You'd be surprised how little water it takes when you conserve this way.

The hot water tank on even the smallest RV will provide enough hot water for one comfy shower before heating up again for the next one. And when brief "Navy" showers are taken, one tank of hot water will be easily adequate for many showers, depending on how efficient the bather controls the water flow.

Is there anything I need to know about using the stove in my RV?

Yes. When using the gas stove or oven, be sure a window or air vent is cracked somewhere. The propane needs a source of air besides what's inside the rig. This is important.

. . .

How do I light an RV's stove?

Although some stoves have a pilot light, most RVers, with the exception of those who stay in one location a long time, keep it off and simply light the burners with either a match or a special butane lighter available for a few dollars at RV supply stores or big box stores.

Many newer stoves have piezoelectric spark lighters for the stovetop burners; just turn on the gas to ignite the spark.

Do I need to be hooked up to electricity for my RV's refrigerator to work?

Sometimes. Most refrigerators will operate on either regular 120-volt AC household electric power or propane.

"Three-way" RV refrigerators will also operate on 12-volt DC power but use so much battery power they're best only operated on DC when the motorhome engine is operating.

If you're towing a travel trailer, the wiring coming from the tow vehicle's alternator is often too small to carry the current required for an RV refrigerator, and the fridge will draw off the trailer's "house" batteries, leaving you in the lurch when you arrive at your destination.

I've heard that my RV must be level for the refrigerator to work. Is this true?

Yes, to run at its maximum capacity. If operated in a severely lopsided position for prolonged periods, the refrigerator may stop cooling and even be permanently damaged.

This is not as big a concern with newer RVs, but it's critical on older units, where the damage may involve a very costly repair. Generally, try to keep the bubble in your leveler at least two-thirds inside the circle.

Can I leave my RV's refrigerator running on propane while traveling?

While some RVers do, it's highly recommended to turn it off while moving, and even better to turn off the propane at its tank. However, if you have a three-way refrigerator and are operating on DC power, then no problem.

By all means, never leave the refrigerator running on propane at a gas station. If vapor blows across the fridge's pilot light it could blow up your RV and everything and everybody in it — plus the gas station. This has happened on more than one occasion. For years, a gas station in Lone Pine, Calif., posted pictures of such an incident — not a pretty sight.

I see a lot of RVs with residential refrigerators. Are they better than the traditional absorption versions?

This is a controversial topic among RVers. Since residential refrigerators require 120 volts AC ("shore power"), they are best used at campgrounds that provide shore power.

Some RVers have managed to use them in a boondocking situation by having enough solar panels, storage batteries, and a properly-sized power inverter.

It can also be difficult (if not impossible) to get a residential refrigerator in an RV serviced when it breaks down. RV technicians, as a rule, do not repair residential refrigerators, and residential refrigerator technicians do not as a rule make service calls to RVs.

One source tells us that residential refrigerators tend to be susceptible to bumps and vibrations on the road, and are known to have a working life of a couple of years when installed in an RV.

What should I do with my refrigerator when I am not using my motorhome?

Turn it off, of course. Remove all food and thoroughly wipe all inside surfaces to clean any residual — but unseen — food particles or spills. Be sure to prop open the doors to avoid mildew and odor buildup.

Do standard bed sheets fit RV beds?

Not necessarily. Just because a manufacturer says a particular coach has a queen-size bed, do not assume it's the same size as your queen bed back home. RV beds are not created equal.

Before buying sheets, measure the bed. You may have to visit a specialty RV store to buy the proper-sized sheets. A product called adjustable bed sheet straps can help secure oversized sheets, so that's an option.

How do RVers do their laundry?

Most use a coin laundry. Most RV parks have at least a few washers and dryers, but sometimes you need to stop at a commercial laundromat.

Many seasonal or full-time RVers in larger coaches have built-in washer-dryers. They have very limited capacity, but they do the job.

Can I use an electric blanket on my bed?

Yes, as long as you are hooked up to electricity. Some RVers use a 12-volt mattress pad instead, which goes beneath the bedding, not on top.

Turning it on about 15 minutes before bedtime makes a bed very cozy when it's time to climb in. These pads draw about seven amps an hour when warming up — about the same as two incandescent light bulbs — but only 20 percent of that amount through the night, making it possible to keep them on until morning (providing you have well-charged deep cycle batteries). Some mattress pad models will operate on either household or 12-volt current at the flip of a switch.

A good way to stay warm on a cold night besides using an electric blanket or other covers is to wear a wool stocking cap. You'd be amazed how much this will warm you up.

Another option is using a *pure* sine-wave inverter with a 120-volt homestyle electric blanket. Using a cheaper, modified sine-wave inverter will often permanently damage an electric blanket control.

Can I blow a fuse in my RV like at home?

Yes. So be sure you know the location of your fuse box and to pack along extra fuses. Your RV probably also has a circuit breaker panel, perhaps with the fuses. Learn where they are and how to reset them in case one cuts out.

How does the heater work in an RV?

In most RVs, the heat from a propane-fueled furnace is circulated through the coach with an electric fan. It will run on 12-volt power when you are not hooked up to utilities, but be aware that the fan draws a lot of power and will drain a deep cycle battery (or two) fairly fast if left on for hours on end. So use your heater very conservatively.

Some RVers install a catalytic heater for use when dry camping. These units require no electricity, but do require some fresh air for combustion, so leave a window or vent cracked. They can also be bumped into easily, resulting in burns, so avoid installing one of these when small children are along.

To save propane when hooked up, some folks bring along a portable electric heater. While many campgrounds say they charge extra for using such a heater, you will almost never be asked when checking in if you plan to run one.

Be careful: Many fires are caused by space heaters. Never use a space heater in conjunction with an extension cord.

.   .   .

**I'd like to travel and earn some money along the way?
How can I learn more about this?**

Workamper News (workamper.com) is the best source of
information about jobs for RVers — and there are plenty of
them out there. Visit its website to learn more.

What's a camp host? How can I become one?

Camp hosts are usually volunteer campers, most often
retired couples, who stay for a month or more (usually a few
months) in their RV at both public campgrounds and
commercial RV parks to keep an eye on things and do
minimal odd jobs.

In return, they will generally receive a free campsite,
most often with hookups even if other sites don't have them.
On some occasions, they may even receive money, but not
much, although the pay is better now than a few years ago.

We met a work camping couple recently who were
camped for the summer at a National Forest campground in
northwest Washington. As is often the case nowadays, the
campground was managed by a private company rather
than the Forest Service.

This couple received a free campsite plus $700 a month.
Workamper News is a good source for locating these positions, which are available across the United States, mostly at
public campgrounds.

You can also check the websites of individual U.S.
National Forests or state parks. In the summer vacation
season, all but small or remote campgrounds have hosts.

I have a business that I'd like to take on the road, but I wonder about working space in my RV.

A lot of RVers operate a business from a motorhome or other RV, and seem to find the space to do it.

Some large RVs come equipped with computer desks, which are helpful. But most RVers do quite well using their dinettes as office desks.

It's relatively easy these days for many people to work from the road. Cell phones, laptop computers and easy access to the Internet enables many RVers to work from wherever they are.

Do I need special vehicle insurance if I'm operating a business from my RV?

You may. Check with your insurance agent. Even monetizing videos you post to YouTube may be viewed by an insurance company as a business.

Be very careful about getting this right if you plan to work from your RV on the road.

. . .

I have heard about jobs where you drive motorhomes from the factory to the dealer and get paid. Is this true? Is it easy to get these jobs?

Yes, it's true. If you think about it, you'll realize that you never see a motorhome or large fifth-wheel trailer being transported on a big truck like you do cars, vans or other smaller vehicles.

Manufacturers and dealers hire drivers — usually regular folks, not professionals — to transport these vehicles. Payment is typically made by the mile and there are some perks, like the potential on one way trips where you may be paid to fly home, picking up frequent flier miles in the process.

Beware, however, that if you use your truck to transport a towable RV to its destination, you'll likely be paid only to the delivery — and nothing for your return trip.

Some "transporters" say it's a great hobby and a way to see the country, but not something you'll ever get rich doing. There is actually quite a demand for people to drive RVs.

If you like to drive and have a good driving record, you might want to check into it. Look for ads soliciting drivers in RV magazines. The Facebook Group RV Transporters is a good source to monitor for information.

In terms of dealing with an emergency on the road, would a CB be worth having along?

A CB is really only helpful when you are in a highly populated area, or along a busy highway. A cell phone, on the other hand, has infinite range.

Still, there are many "black holes," where a cellular phone cannot pick up a signal. If you want to cover all your bases, bring a cell phone AND a CB or high-powered walkie-talkie.

I'm single. I am concerned that I would get lonely without a companion.

It can be lonely, for sure, but a lot of singles travel by RV and are very happy. To learn more about the single RV lifestyle and meet other single RVers, consider joining Loners On Wheels. Get information from the group's website LonersOnWheels.com.

Many RVers report that having a dog along helps keep the blues away.

I'm a single woman and am a bit worried about traveling by myself. Do you have any suggestions or words of encouragement?

Yes, thousands upon thousands of single, widowed or otherwise solo women are traveling America in RVs.

The best source of information on this subject is through the club RVing Women at https://www.RVing-women.org.

I plan to bring a firearm with me on my RV trips. Is this okay?

About 40 percent of RVers tell us they carry a firearm all or part of the time. If you travel with one, here are a few things to keep in mind: Don't take a weapon into Canada or Mexico unless you have a good reason and have researched the laws.

When crossing a state border, be sure you are not in

violation of the gun laws in the state you're entering: what's legal in one state may be a felony in another.

If you plan to travel extensively with a firearm, be sure to get the annual guide book, "Traveler's Guide to the Firearm Laws of the 50 States." A new edition is published every January.

My husband and I plan to go full-time. We enjoy several TV programs and don't want to miss them. What should we do?

Sign up for a satellite service. The receiving dishes are small and inexpensive these days and will enable you to receive up to hundreds of stations from wherever you are for a monthly fee that's comparable to your home cable TV service.

Many RVers use DirectTV. The satellite dish can either be portable or be permanently installed on the roof of your RV.

How do I get access to my bank accounts while on the road?

Virtually all RVers have an ATM debit card that they can use at automatic teller machines almost anywhere they go, often for free but sometimes for a fee of two or three dollars.

Most banks offer online banking which makes banking from the road almost as easy as at home. All you need is an Internet connection and your PIN.

Many banks offer an app that enables you to deposit checks using your smartphone. Check with your own bank to see if it offers a good program and, if not, check around until you find one you like.

Are travelers checks a good idea, too?

In our opinion, travelers checks are as archaic as dinosaurs. They are not necessary.

What about getting mail while on the road?

Many mail forwarding services will send along your mail for a small fee. Some RVers have their mail sent to a relative who forwards it on.

Some big RV clubs offer mail forwarding services. Both the Family Motor Coaching Association and the Escapees offer economical and popular programs. We highly recommend Americas Mailbox in South Dakota.

If you don't frequent RV parks but prefer boondocking, your mail can be sent to a local post office through their General Delivery service. There's no cost for this, but it's best to call ahead for details — some offices have limited General Delivery pick-up hours.

Is traveling with a pet a good idea?

It's common and popular. Most campgrounds and RV parks allow pets. Some private ones will charge a fee per pet or even not accept some aggressive breeds. Most have strict leash laws.

But always remember when traveling with pets to be considerate of your fellow campers. If you bring along a dog that barks a lot when lonely, do not leave it alone. The noise will spoil the solitude of nearby campers. And please *pick up* after your dog.

Do I need an awning for my rig?

If you spend a lot of time in the desert, other hot places, or in rainy climates, then it's a good idea.

An awning also adds a "porch" to your RV, which many RVers enjoy. Awnings are standard equipment on most trailers and larger motorhomes.

Are awnings hard to set up and take down?

No. On many Class A coaches they are fully automatic. On most other RVs it's a fairly simple routine: Release the locking lever and latches, use the awning rod to pull down on the strap and unroll the awning, lock in the rafter arms and then raise the main arms. Taking them down is just the reverse.

Don't awnings flap in the wind?

They can, but inexpensive "de-flappers" are available to reduce wind noise.

.   .   .

Wouldn't an awning get torn apart in a storm?

If there's a chance of strong winds or heavy rain, it's best to retract your awning. We know one couple who returned to their rig on a clear, sunny day and found their awning flipped right over the top of their rig — an unexpected wind gust did serious damage.

Some electrically deployed awnings have wind sensors that automatically retract themselves if an unsafe wind speed is reached.

For manual awnings, tie-down straps can be used, too, that place a strap over the entire width of the awning and anchor into the ground at both ends.

Does rain pose any danger to an awning?

Absolutely! Heavy rains, if not allowed to shed off an awning, can cause it to act like a large water reservoir. The weight of the water has been known by some unfortunate RVers to actually bend and break awning arms.

If there's a chance of rain, it's best to set the awning to a tilted angle, which will prevent rainwater from collecting on the awning fabric.

I'm an avid fisherman and plan to travel in my new motorhome throughout the United States. Is there a national fishing license?

No. But there are two options that come to mind. First, you can always buy a short-term license in each state you visit. These may only be a few dollars for a few days. Another option is to seek out the many RV parks with private fishing lakes.

Because the lakes (most often ponds) are on the campground's property with no public streams feeding them, you can fish without a state license.

In some parks, you can keep what you catch with no charge; in others you pay by the fish or by the pound. In many campgrounds there is no charge to fish, but if you catch something you'll need to toss it back.

You may get lucky by Googling "free fishing day in (name of state)." Most states have at least one day each year when you can fish without a state license.

I keep hearing RVers talk about the Slabs. What is it?

The Slabs is short for Slab City, an old military installation in the desert alongside the Salton Sea in Southern California, about four miles east of the town of Niland.

Camping is free and thousands of RVers in rigs of all shapes, sizes and road-worthiness hole up there every winter (too hot in the summer). They socialize, hold flea markets, and even have their own CB "radio station."

The Slabs, with its hodgepodge crowd, is not for everyone, but it's worth an overnight stay just to witness this often colorful RV subculture.

·　·　·

I also hear a lot about a place called Quartzsite in Arizona. What's there?

Quartzsite, Ariz., is just east of the California border along I-10 in what was, until recently, the middle of nowhere. Now, in the winter season, it's the site of a huge and nearly non-stop flea market and gem show.

RVers in all types and sizes of rigs hole up in and around town for free on public lands or in inexpensive RV parks.

At peak times, tens of thousands of RVers may be in the area. It's an amazing sight and a worthwhile destination for any RVer who seeks bargains, free or inexpensive camping, sunshine and clean desert air. A free RV show is held each January in a giant tent and draws huge crowds.

7

FULL-TIME RVING

Is it legal to live in an RV full-time?

Yes and no. The RV Industry Association, which regulates RV standards, says that RVs are intended for "temporary living."

But people live in them year-round full-time anyway without any issues. At least so far. This could change.

There is no law against it on a national level, but most municipalities have laws that prevent full-time RV living in their jurisdictions.

Is it really feasible to retire in an RV?

Yes, and more and more people are doing it every day, joining the hundreds of thousands of RVers who have already sold their homes to travel full-time.

An excellent group for full-time RVers is the Escapees (https://www.Escapees.com). Benefits include an excellent newsletter, mail forwarding service, regional and national get-togethers, local and special interest chapters, and a network of member-owned campgrounds and "boon-docking sites" where members can stay at very low rates.

Contact the Escapees at 100 Rainbow Drive, Livingston, TX 77351, or call 936-327-8873.

I plan to go full-time for a year and will probably buy a fifth wheel trailer. What is the minimum size I will need to be comfortable?

There is no definitive answer. We see full-timers in huge RVs — whether fifth wheels, travel trailers or motorhomes — and yet others get by in relatively small units — 24 feet or less.

Some full-timers swear they need at least 30 feet of RV or they'll be at each other's throats, and yet others say they are perfectly happy in tighter quarters.

Slideouts, common in most RVs these days, provide a lot of extra space, making day-to-day living more comfortable.

Our suggestion is to explore many, many units of different lengths, and talk with current full-timers about what works for them. Single RVers, of course, will most often need less space.

We don't know what to do with our house and our "stuff" when we go full-time. What do other full-timers do?

Everybody does it differently. Some just lock up their homes while they're gone. Others find a housesitter. Others rent their home for a year or two while they travel with their RV.

Some sell their home, get rid of most of their possessions and store what's left in a rental storage unit. There is no one way to do this. Just do what works for you.

. . .

When we tell our friends we are going full-time, they tell us we are nuts. Our kids think we have lost our marbles. Are we really crazy to even consider traveling full-time in an RV?

No, as most full-timers would tell you if you asked them. It's very common, however, for friends and family to have a tough time accepting such a huge lifestyle change in those close to them.

Kids might worry about their parents' safety or the absence of Grandma and Grandpa from their own children. Friends might even be envious. But determined, would-be full-timers follow their instincts and seldom have regrets.

My wife and I get along great, but we wonder how we would do in a confined space if we went full-time.

This is important to consider. It's pretty obvious that even in a large RV, a couple will not have as much personal space as in a regular house.

Some couples, upon hitting the road full-time, discover they do not get along well in such close proximity. Others thrive.

A good idea before selling the house is to take a long test trip to see how well you get along. If you end up wanting to strangle each other on a regular basis, stick to weekend outings.

My husband and I have a lot of friends where we live now. We wonder if full-time RVers make friends in their travels or if they are pretty much on their own?

Interestingly, most full-timers who are not loners by nature make many friends as they travel, often meeting up with them again and again.

Some RVers form caravans to travel from place to place. One thing you seldom hear full-timers complaining about is a lack of friends.

My husband and I are retired. He wants to sell the house, buy a big fifth wheel trailer and travel in it full-time. I enjoyed our short camping trips years ago with our children, but am scared to death about traveling full-time. So we're having some pretty heated discussions. He's halfway out the door, but I'm dragging my feet. Do you have any advice?

With most couples, one person will want to go more than the other, most often the husband. Sometimes it's a question of one wanting to go full-time, the other part-time. Sometimes it's one wanting to sell the house, and the other wanting to keep it.

We can't answer what's best for you and your husband. But keep talking. Perhaps taking a trial run of a few months might allow this question to resolve itself.

I am in my 30s. Will I just be around a lot of old people in campgrounds?

Actually, millennials make up more than a third of campground users, according to a 2019 industry survey, and are a common sight everywhere you go.

You will have no problem finding people your own age where you camp. And, heck, older folks, aren't aliens: they'll provide you with lots of company, maybe even try to spoil you.

During the pandemic of 2020, many millennials purchased RVs and are staying in campgrounds, so the percentage may even be higher than a third now.

My wife and I have two children, both in elementary school. We really want to RV full-time, but wonder if it's feasible to homeschool our kids.

More and more RVing families are doing this, using traditional homeschooling methods as well as those via the Internet.

We don't know the figures, but a significant number of children are on the road full-time with their parents, being homeschooled as they go. You might want to consider joining the group Fulltime Families at fulltimefamilies.com.

Do I need special insurance if I live in my RV full-time?

Some policies will cover you, but some won't. Be sure to talk to your agent and then read the fine print in your policy.

If your policy does not cover full-time living and you are in a serious accident, your insurance company can deny your claim, which could wipe out your life savings.

Do RV parks have special rates for full-timers?

Many parks offer weekly, monthly and seasonal rates, which will provide significant savings over the day rate. Some will allow you to stay year-round, but you're essentially living in a "trailer park" then.

MISCELLANEOUS QUESTIONS

I want to take my large family on an RV trip, and am interested in renting a large Class A motorhome rather than a Class C, which seems to be the standard rental unit. Can you recommend a good place?

Try El Monte RV or Cruise America, both of which have locations around the states. They rent both Class C and Class A motorhomes.

Get info on the web at ElMonteRV.com or CruiseAmerica.com. As an alternative, you can rent an RV from private owners through a referral agency, too.

In addition, a number of peer-to-peer rental services exist, allowing RV owners to rent out their rigs to others.

My husband and I want to travel full-time in an RV, but I am very sensitive to chemicals and cannot tolerate strong scents. Does the smell of the propane or smoke from campfires get inside the RV?

You should never smell any LP gas inside your rig at any time, even when running the furnace or generator, unless there's a malfunction (in which case get your system checked immediately as propane is nothing to fool with).

You will have to be selective about your campgrounds, though, as it can be impossible to keep campfire smoke out. Many private campgrounds do not allow campfires, so there will be no problem there.

But public campgrounds, like those in National Parks and National Forests, can be terribly smoky on summer evenings, when everyone wants to roast marshmallows by the campfire.

If the evening is warm, you'll swelter without your windows open (and using the air conditioning for anything but a short burst of time is not appropriate at these places because it involves running the generator), so the smoke will pour right in.

The RV itself, too, might be your biggest problem. Chemicals and glues used in materials will linger for a long time in a new unit and there can be other fumes from exhaust, toilet chemicals, etc.

In the previous answer, you said it's not appropriate to run a generator in National Park and National Forest campgrounds. What do you mean? Is this a law?

No, it's not necessarily a law, but a rule in some campgrounds. In these pristine places, it's incredibly rude to run a noisy generator (and they all make some noise) except for brief periods during the day.

Your neighbors will likely be there on vacation, and forcing them to listen to engine noise rather than the sounds of nature is just plain inconsiderate. In most National Parks and many other public campgrounds, hours will be posted when it's okay to run a generator.

I've heard some RVers call their large motorhome's "buses." Are their RVs bus conversions?

Sometimes. But more likely they are the owners of the biggest and most expensive motorhomes, called motor coaches, built on a bus chassis.

The cost of these "palaces on wheels" is usually $300,000 and up, some more than a million dollars.

What if my motorhome has mechanical problems on the road? Is it easy to find a repair shop?

It can be, but very often it is not. If the RV's engine is

American made, you might want to head (or limp) to the nearest dealer, but be warned that some will not work on motorhomes which are too big for their shops.

If the problem is with the "home" part of the rig, look for a dealer that sells your brand of RV, but be aware that the dealer may be too busy to get you in for repairs for weeks, even longer. Some dealers, sad to say, will not even work on an RV that was not purchased at its dealership.

A general RV repair shop is another choice or, even better, a mobile RV service. In remote areas, however, finding a good repair shop can be a challenge.

Your best bet is to fix the problem yourself. It helps very much to be handy if you travel with an RV, and carry a well stocked tool box.

I just bought a 9-year-old motorhome in mint condition with original tires that look like new. But I've heard I should replace the tires. Is this necessary?

Our RVtravel.com tire expert advises that RV tire life is not based so much on tread wear but, rather, on age.

The lifespan of motorhome tires is probably a safe seven years, but certainly no more than ten. For "towable" units like travel trailers and fifth wheels, getting three to five safe years out of tires is the safest call. You can have a tire dealer pull and inspect your tires.

If worse comes to worst, if you blow a tire on your motorhome, your reaction behind the wheel may save your life.

Here's a good film from Michelin tires about dealing with a blowout. https://www.michelinrvtires.com/tires/tires-101/tire-maintenance-and-safety/how-to-handle-a-blowout/

Name three things I can do to help my RV live longer.

Change the engine oil regularly, make sure the coach is not overloaded and that the tires are properly inflated, and have the roof inspected at least once a year for potential leaks.

Can I use an RV in the winter?

Absolutely. Take it to the Southwest deserts, Florida, or the Texas Hill Country (or even Baja), where you will be among thousands of other RVers seeking the sun.

Or take it skiing, in which case you'll need to take special precautions against freezing the water system. This may mean modifying your use of onboard water, including not using the freshwater tank at all.

What about shopping on the road? Isn't it hard getting into parking lots?

For Class A coaches, motorhomes towing a dinghy or

anyone pulling a trailer, parking lots can be challenging. Experienced RVers scope out problematic lots before entering to make sure there's an easy exit and that there is likely to be enough space for the rig.

Most of the time you will need to take at least two parking slots, end-to-end, or up to six or more if you have to park crosswise, so don't hog prime spots for shoppers. You'll find more room to park farther away from the main entrance and you're less likely to upset other shoppers. Use Google Earth or Google Maps for aerial and street views of where you are headed.

Isn't there an awful lot to learn and remember?

It can seem daunting at first. Many RVers put together checklists to help them remember everything. It also helps to follow routines. Do things in the same order each time and try to avoid distractions. For example, don't stop to chat while you are hitching up your trailer or toad. Finish the job, then tell your neighbor farewell.

· · ·

Can you explain RV "weight information"?

Every manufacturer includes weight rating information, often on a sticker or certificate. Here's what all that information means.

GVWR – Gross Vehicle Weight Rating: The maximum total weight of a motorhome or trailer and its contents as allowed by the manufacturer's engineering. For safety it's critical not to exceed this weight.

GCWR – Gross Combined Weight Rating: The maximum total combined weight of the tow vehicle plus anything towed. This is a good gauge of how well the vehicle will tow in terms of muscle. The closer your total weight gets to this number, the tougher towing performance can become.

GAWR – Gross Axle Weight Rating: The maximum weight that can be carried by the axle, including tires and wheels.

UVW – Unloaded Vehicle Weight: Also known as "dry weight," this is the claimed weight of a motorhome or trailer as it rolls off the manufacturer's line. What's added after that, by the dealer or a previous owner, affects that weight.

NCC – Net Carrying Capacity: The amount of weight you can add in terms of gear, food, water, sewage, even passengers. NCC is found in older rigs, but has been replaced recently by a couple of other terms, which follow.

SCWR – Sleeping Capacity Weight Rating: The manufacturer's designated number of sleeping positions multiplied by 154 pounds (70 kilograms).

CCC – Cargo Carrying Capacity: This is the "new" description of Net Carrying Capacity, but doesn't include the weight of fresh water, LP gas, oil, and engine fuel. It's a complicated formula. GVWR minus UVW, and minus the

weight of full fresh (potable) water (including that in the
water heater), the weight of full LP-gas, and SCWR.

FIND MORE RV INFORMATION AT WWW.RVTRAVEL.COM.

*SUBSCRIBE TO THE RV TRAVEL NEWSLETTER: HTTPS://WWW.
RVTRAVEL.COM/SUBSCRIBE/*

Made in the USA
Monee, IL
21 October 2020

45814738R00075